ADVANCE PRAISE FOR

Context Blindness: Digital Technology and the Next Stage of Human Evolution

"At once a penetrating social analysis and an eloquent lament for where we are now and where we may be headed, this book is required reading for anyone who wants to understand the source of our failings and delusions. Dr. Berger presents a clear, cogent, and concise diagnosis of the ills of present-day culture, one that is essential if we are to begin to seek healing by reclaiming our real, human contexts once more."

—Douglas Rushkoff, Author, *Present Shock* and *Team Human*

"In this provocative and highly accessible book, Eva Berger identifies caetexia as a major malady of today's times, one that bears a wide array of personal, social and political symptoms. Her abundant examples and theoretical connections allow readers to see key patterns across many different changes occurring throughout the contemporary world. In identifying context blindness as an unanticipated evolutionary consequence of digital media, Berger makes our fragmented, disconnected, and perplexing world more intelligible and more understandable. Tom Wolfe famously asked of Marshall McLuhan's work, 'What if he is right?' I could not help but think along the same lines regarding Berger's bold and sobering work here: 'What if she is right?'"

—Corey Anton, Vice-President of the Institute of General Semantics,
Professor of Communication Studies, Grand Valley State University

"This is an urgent, stirring, and relevant book. It revives media theory that has been unjustly pushed aside in the digital age and focuses on some of the most interesting challenges we face."

—Siva Vaidhyanathan, Author, *Antisocial Media: How Facebook Disconnects Us and Undermines Democracy*

"In *Context Blindness*, Dr. Eva Berger presents a persuasive case that human beings, shaped by the media environments we have created, are evolving to a species that will not or cannot attend to the contexts we inhabit. Our ever-present connection to the internet that first intruded upon our sacred spaces (family dinner, classrooms, and churches) has now simply erased our understanding of how behaviors and spaces might differ. This erasure has replaced questions about what subjects and actions are appropriate in a specific context with arguments about trigger warnings and safe spaces—ultimately making no space safe. The algorithms that rule our lives are encouraging cancel culture and blinding us to the very idea of perspective. With an artful and passionate prose, Berger has issued a warning that the toxic human behaviors we are observing may be a natural selection provoked by our own inventions."

—Missy Alexander, Provost, Western Connecticut State University

Context Blindness

UNDERSTANDING
MEDIA
ECOLOGY

Lance Strate
General Editor

Vol. 10

The Understanding Media Ecology series is part
of the Peter Lang Media and Communication list.
Every volume is peer reviewed and meets
the highest quality standards for content and production.

PETER LANG
New York • Bern • Berlin
Brussels • Vienna • Oxford • Warsaw

Eva Berger

Context Blindness

Digital Technology and the Next Stage of Human Evolution

PETER LANG
New York • Bern • Berlin
Brussels • Vienna • Oxford • Warsaw

Library of Congress Cataloging-in-Publication Control Number: 2021047328

Bibliographic information published by **Die Deutsche Nationalbibliothek.**
Die Deutsche Nationalbibliothek lists this publication in the "Deutsche Nationalbibliografie"; detailed bibliographic data are available on the Internet at http://dnb.d-nb.de/.

ISSN 2374-7676 (print)
ISSN 2374-7684 (online)
ISBN 978-1-4331-8613-4 (hardcover)
ISBN 978-1-4331-8614-1 (ebook pdf)
ISBN 978-1-4331-8615-8 (epub)
DOI 10.3726/b18145

80 Broad Street, 5th floor, New York, NY 10004
www.peterlang.com

For my parents, Isaac and Zlate
—among the last vestiges of Homo sapiens, trying to wrap their heads around it all—
with love

Table of Contents

Preface

They say we should let go of our grudges. That they are no good for us. That harboring anger and other negative feelings can end up hurting us. On the other hand, I was taught that there is nothing like a grudge to spark interesting research; that the research process, as well as the result, are the most meaningful if you care about your topic, especially if it makes you mad.

This book came about as a result of a huge grudge. Not the kind of bitterness one holds onto way too long after a precipitating incident, but a deep, persistent, ongoing feeling of anger, disbelief, and astonishment at the number of precipitating incidents and the frequency of their occurrence over the past few years.

I became obsessed with finding an encompassing explanation to seemingly unrelated events, some in my professional life and my direct experience, and others in the world, mediated by television and social media.

In my professional life as a college professor, I was startled by a new kind of student who obviously had a new definition and understanding of college and its purpose, different from that of generations that came before them. Their behavior felt rude, their language and demeanor seemed not to fit the situation.

In the realm of politics, Trump's presidency was one of the primary triggers. His daily nonsensical utterances, rage, and vengeance were mindboggling and kept everyone thinking about politics all the time and constantly on edge. And, as Sullivan (2017) put it, "one of the great achievements of a free society in a stable democracy is that many people, for much of the time, need not think about politics at all."

I envisioned people's reactions to Trump's posts and tweets on social media as if we were all a colossal amoeba, moving left and right to the slightest stimulus of touch or light. As if we had been reduced to bytes ourselves. Conglomerations of cells reacting to stimuli as they come, without a memory of the past or thoughts about the future. Without a context. Like emojis, smiling, crying, liking, or disliking, as signal reactions to whatever is trending.

My sense of helplessness increased with the mounting polarization worldwide, immigration crises, phenomena such as cancel culture, and cries of cultural appropriation. There was also the less than insidious and very palpably past-the-tipping-point global warming. And COVID-19, of course. Dystopian television series such as *Black Mirror*, *The Handmaid's Tale*, and *Years and Years* felt like documentaries.

As we kept going down our ever-deepening rabbit holes, all our feeds became dominated by fringe ideas and conspiracy theories. If we watched one video on YouTube, we started to get recommendations that were all on the same topic as the original one, as if the algorithm thought that the subject of that original video was our life's obsession.

I embarked on a journey to find an explanation for the madness around me, and I found it. This book is about the idea that since we have delegated the ability to read context to the algorithms of contextual technologies such as social media, location, and sensors, we have become context-blind. And that our context blindness could be the harbinger of the next stage of human evolution.

I have stopped obsessing. But deep concern has replaced the grudge.

References

Sullivan, A. (February 10, 2017). The madness of King Donald. *New York Magazine*.

Acknowledgments

I can only begin by acknowledging Lance Strate for his help and support throughout the years. He is this book's series editor, colleague, friend, and role model of scholarship generally and in media ecology specifically.

I thank Andrew Postman for his encouragement and advice, belief in the book, and help to fine-tune its thesis at the very early stages.

My gratitude to Aliza Savir, my friend and fellow media ecologist, whose reaction to the idea for the book finally sent me to sit down and start writing. Her feedback along the way has been invaluable.

I want to thank Michael Gibson, my editor at Peter Lang, and express my appreciation for my colleagues Dan Arav and Yuval Dror for their support. I also want to acknowledge my friends Ariel Ben-Porath and Dorit Naaman, for their helpful comments along the way.

I am indebted to my son Etai for his original thought, creative ideas, and elucidations; to my son Jonathan for his intelligent, quiet, and unassuming insights; and my nephew Shay for his prolific research, bright illuminations, and assistance. Somewhere at the border between Millennials and Gen Zers, the three are heartwarmingly, perhaps miraculously, the opposite of context-blind.

Finally, I am grateful to and for Yuval, my sounding board, loving critic, partner, and best friend since 1980.

Introduction

Every era in human history has a defining disease, and the language used around every disease defines the response of both patients and society to that disease. The illness itself then becomes a metaphor to describe unrelated social processes and cultural phenomena that resemble the symptoms—or the stigma—of the disease: cancer must be "fought" or "defeated," and hatred is "like a cancer."

Due to the physical disfigurement that accompanies leprosy, the sick suffered humiliation and segregation, and the word "leper" became synonymous with an outcast or a pariah. As Susan Sontag (2001) explains, tuberculosis was initially viewed as a disease of the artist afflicting a person of sensitive and sad temperament, and later as a product of urban decay and sexual excess. Similarly, AIDS became a symbol for social disorder and moral decadence. Neil Postman (1992) compares information glut—the overload of information that leads to the breakdown of a coherent cultural narrative—to AIDS. The dangers of information on the loose, he explains, are like those of an impaired immune system that cannot manage cellular growth and destroy unwanted cells.

Disease is the metaphorical source for psychological states as well. We can be "lovesick," we buy things we don't need because "nobody is immune to advertising," and unexceptional events are "like the common cold." We talk about behaviors as contagious, like laughter or riots. We draw parallels between the spreading of germs and the spreading of ideas.

The term "contagion" is used to explain phenomena in economics (financial contagion), psychology (social contagion), and anthropology (cultural contagion); we use it to describe the spread of ideas within social networks in the real world and online as well (Mitchell, 2012). We also speak about "viral" memes, Facebook posts, and advertising campaigns. The source of this metaphor has become more physically tangible, of course, since the COVID-19 pandemic. One may wonder whether its application to computers and social media has stripped it of its malign associations, making it difficult for us to see viruses as the potentially lethal, biological phenomena that they are. As Susan Sontag (2001) suggests, metaphors of illness obstruct the rational awareness necessary to contain disease. Our impaired ability to think of the coronavirus as literal may partly explain the arguments over masks and social distancing that facilitated its spread, although we never politicized anti-virus software or claimed it infringed on our liberties.

Every generation, it seems, has a defining physical or psychological illness. When the condition's characteristics are made public by popular science, we all begin to use them as explanations for our own or others' behavior. The rise in popularity of reality television, and with it the quest for instant celebrity, made "narcissistic personality disorder" the diagnosis of the moment. Then came "OCD," "ADD," "bipolar," and "borderline," and today "autistic" and "Asperger's" are the most commonly quoted and loosely used terms by laypersons to describe (often in a demeaning manner) the socially awkward friend or ex-spouse, the friendless child, or the abusive boss (Wallace, 2012).

This use of the term autism is, of course, unfair to those indeed afflicted by the condition because when it becomes a slur, it leads to stereotyping and to the misunderstanding of the challenges and needs autistic people must face. In this book, it is meant neither as an actual medical diagnosis nor as an insult, of course. Autism seems to be the most useful metaphor to describe the human condition at the start of the third decade of the twenty-first century.

One of the most dominant manifestations of autistic behavior at the highest levels of the autistic spectrum is context blindness, or *caetextia* in Latin (Caetextia, 2009). People with autism assign meaning in an absolute way and not in a context-specific way. This affects abilities such as face perception, recognition of emotions, understanding language and communication, and problem-solving.

As it turns out, not only people with autism have difficulty reading facial expressions and recognizing emotions. A study conducted by UCLA (Morin, 2014) found that digital media decreased children's ability to read other people's feelings. Social skills require practice, and we had been low on this practice for a while when the pandemic struck. We were looking at our phones an average of

96 times daily in 2019 (Asurion Research, 2019) but most of our conversations in 2020 took place behind a screen, and chances are that our ability to socialize in-person has been even further compromised. With muted screens on Zoom, we have become used to an unnatural silence and absence of conversation fillers (such as "uh" and "um"). Some are finding face-to-face conversations awkward and less fluid and their online behavior leaking into their real lives.

In addition, the social distancing and wearing of face masks imposed by the COVID-19 pandemic may turn out to have negative implications for babies and their bonding, early attachment, and connections with others (Green et al., 2020). It is much harder to read people's emotions behind masks, and if we can't read other people's emotions, empathy deteriorates too.

When people with autism find it hard to empathize, it is because their brain lacks contextual sensitivity. They are affected by context blindness. It is important to emphasize, however, as Strate (2006) points out, that autistics' lack of empathy does not imply antipathy, nor does autistic alienation necessarily lead to immoral conduct. As Frith (in Strate, 2006) explains:

> Some of the perceived abnormalities of autistic social behavior can be seen not so much as impairments, but as unusually positive qualities. These qualities can be captured by terms such as innocence, honesty, and guilelessness. Autistic people are not adept at deceiving others, nor at impressing others. They are not manipulative or gossipy…they are not envious and can give to others gladly…. Autistic people may not empathize in the common sense of the word, but neither do they gloat over other people's misfortune. Indeed, they can be profoundly upset by the suffering they see, and they can show righteous indignation. (p. 120)

The eroded contextual sensitivity that seems to be afflicting us all explains at least some of the lack of empathy we have seen around us over the past few years. Context blindness explains former U.S. President Donald Trump's lack of empathy. It explains how this unorthodox demagogue who challenged all the conventions of modern-day politics, a brash celebrity-turned-politician who used unfiltered talk and defied all norms of public civility, won the U.S. presidential election. When we are blind to context, we cannot be civil, as we don't have the context (cultural or social) to serve as a guide for what is acceptable and what is not when we play a certain role in a given situation. For the context-blind, civil norms are rendered meaningless or transparent. The concept of common sense ethics disappears, as there is no *common* sense—no basic shared, self-evident moral principles to guide us.

Context blindness also explains Jair Bolsonaro, current president of Brazil. Upon his return to Brazil from a visit to Israel in 2019, at a meeting with evangelical pastors in Rio de Janeiro, he said that the crimes of the Holocaust are forgivable. In a clarification posted later, he blamed "those who want to push him away from his Jewish friends" for taking his speech out of context. He added that forgiveness is something personal, and his speech was never meant to be used in a historical context. What other context is there when talking about the Holocaust? Well, when there is no understanding of context, you can talk about the Holocaust in whatever context you want—including a personal, Hallmark-card kind of context—and in that context, "good friends always forgive."

Another good example of context blindness is the ultra-orthodox weekly in Israel that blurred the faces of women featured in a famous picture from the Warsaw Ghetto Uprising. The photograph, featuring a Jewish boy holding his hands up in submission, depicts the surrender of Jews after the Uprising. Most of the Jews in the picture were sent to extermination camps. But for the publication, the context of the photograph is invisible, and female Holocaust casualties and survivors are sexual objects, so their faces were blurred, and the little girl walking next to her mother was cropped out completely (Tessler, 2013).

Fake news can also be explained by our inability to understand context. Culture watchers and worriers—everyone who is concerned about the disregard for facts and the rule of emotion over reason—have been trying to understand fake news and the multiple explanations that have been provided for them.

Masha Gessen (2016), for example, explains that fake news and alternative facts are told for the same reason that Vladimir Putin lies: "to assert power over truth itself." Another explanation is that with trusted news establishments in decline, fake news is disseminated faster and wider than ever before through social media such as Twitter or Facebook. Clearly, technology has changed the way that lies, or fake news are communicated. On the Internet, they are clickbait meant to lure us into reading more and to expose us to advertisers' messages. In addition, most traffic to news websites is driven by social networks, and the algorithms of those social networks give us news stories that are trending rather than those that are important or accurate. The algorithms that create news feeds don't care much about journalistic norms. There, user-driven metrics are used, and the "wisdom of the crowd" blurs the lines between fact and opinion (Keen, 2011).

I have attended carefully to these various explanations, and I do not claim that they are wrong or that my explanation is the only one possible, but the lies that come so easily to despots today have always come easily to despots. Totalitarian-leaning leaders always present alternative facts, weakening our ability to make moral judgments. As Hannah Arendt (1973) wrote long before the Internet, "the ideal subject of totalitarian rule...are people for whom the distinction between fact and fiction (i.e., the reality of experience) and the distinction between true and false (i.e., the standards of thought) no longer exist" (p. 474).

There is strong evidence all around us that we have now slipped into an unprecedented reality in most areas of life, and not only in the realm of facts and truth. The insurgence at the U.S. Capitol, the rise of QAnon, and the election of figures like Marjorie Taylor Greene to Congress are not "more of the same," but rather signs of a profound transformation.

My argument here presumes a more all-encompassing grasp of our current human condition, and the value of the argument resides in its media ecological perspective. This perspective has its origins in the observations of authors such as Marshall McLuhan and Neil Postman. Media ecology is the study of media as environments, of environments as media, of the structure of situations or contexts, and it provides the definition of "context" in the context of this book.

Context is a set of conditions involving space, time, objects, symbols, and transactions between people, culture, and reality. The conditions are functions of one another and of the media through which they are conducted, and they allow us to label the situations we find ourselves in. The conditions also enable us to predict how others will behave and their expectations of us. These situations or contexts assign us roles. They tell us who we are. Context helps us concentrate on what is relevant and ignore what is irrelevant. It helps us make sense of the world.

Media ecology is context analysis; thus, it explains our context blindness. Media ecology focuses on the implications of technology and postulates that technological development leads to the creation of new human abilities and the weakening or even disappearance of older abilities. When skills are delegated to technology, unused skills and capacities tend to atrophy.

The advent of automated airplane operation weakened pilots' abilities to respond creatively in emergencies. Pilots these days spend more time learning automated systems than practicing hands-on flying, and they often have trouble manually flying the plane: "They become a systems operator rather than a stick-and-rudder pilot" (Nicas & Wichter, 2019).

Doctors who rely entirely on technology are increasingly losing their ability to make diagnoses based on observation. With their attention focused on the massive amounts of data generated by lab and imaging tests rather than on the patient, they find themselves spending more time at their desks and at their computers than at patients' bedsides. The physical exam is almost a lost art. The skills that legendary physician William Osler called "inspection, palpation, percussion and auscultation" (Zaman, 2018) are barely used. As Abraham Verghese half-jokingly said: "If you come to our hospital missing a finger, no one will believe you until we get a CT scan, an MRI and an orthopedic consult" (Knox, 2010).

As Nicholas Carr (2010) explains:

> When a ditch digger trades his shovel for a backhoe, his arm muscles weaken even as his efficiency increases. A similar trade-off may well take place as we automate the work of the mind…our technologies at once strengthen and sap us. (n.p.)

The animated film *Wall-E* was also about how technology shapes us, about what skills weaken or completely atrophy, about the impact that fully automated systems for food, drink, entertainment, and transportation on an intergalactic spacecraft are having on our lives. The hovering chairs that move humans about in the junkyard that Planet Earth has become lead to atrophy, to loss of agency and skills, to flab. Losing bone density and becoming amorphous blobs are, of course, visible results of atrophy due to the delegation of abilities to work and transportation technologies. The loss of intellectual, cognitive, and social skills as a result of their transfer to media of communication are harder to identify and take longer to notice. In Carr's words again:

> When the power loom was invented, weavers could manufacture far more cloth during the course of a workday than they'd been able to make by hand, but they sacrificed some of their manual dexterity, not to mention some of their "feel" for fabric. Their fingers, in McLuhan's terms, became numb. Farmers, similarly, lost some of their feel for the soil when they began using mechanical harrows and plows...The toll can be particularly high with our intellectual technologies. The tools of the mind amplify and in turn numb the most intimate, the most human, of our natural capacities—those for reason, perception, memory, emotion. (n.p.)

Why perform the basic arithmetic required for splitting a check or calculating the tip for a waiter at a restaurant if we can use the calculator on our phones? Why tell time by the hands of an analog watch if we can quickly look at our phones? Why remember birthdays when our calendars and social media accounts remember them for us? They even provide no-effort templates to say "Happy Birthday" quickly and move on. So, what if we gave up the pleasant feeling that once came with being congratulated by someone who remembered, or at least took the time to write it down to be reminded? Why retain the ability to give instructions if we can tell someone what to type into Waze instead? Why write cursive, or write at all, if one can type? Or talk? We don't need any special skills to take good photographs either. Just add a filter on Instagram and…voila!

Human skills have been delegated to technology throughout history. The invention of writing weakened our biological memory; rational thought was impaired with the advent of television, and contextual technologies of the digital age have made us context-blind.

When GPS decides what route is best and iTunes decides what song to play, humans forget how to contextualize. When we completely outsource all our skills to mobile technology, location services, sensors, social media, and AI, we stop understanding the most basic situations. To relinquish control over our decisions to contextual technology is to give up our awareness of context.

When we live so much of our social lives on social media, we forget how to behave in the real world. We have become really good at distinguishing nuances of emotion between a smiling emoji, a grinning face, a beaming face with smiling eyes, a face with tears of joy or rolling-on-the-floor-laughing. In the physical world, our sensitivities have coarsened. Walking on the street, it has become one's job to evade those walking with their eyes on their phones, not experiencing life, too busy documenting and uploading it to Instagram and walking into elevators before letting others out.

Sitting with a friend at a coffee shop or with our family over dinner, we text and swipe and look at our phones instead of at them. We no longer feel insulted when the people we are conversing with take their eyes off ours, "leaving us" or "putting us on hold."

We are "tethered and marked absent" (Turkle, 2017). In other words, we may be physically present in a situation, but tethered to our mobile devices, we are mentally and emotionally elsewhere. Before the Internet, a "place" was made up of physical space and the people within it. Today, the places we physically inhabit have become invisible to us. They have ceased to provide context for our interactions because we are all physically present but have fixed our attention on the absent and the remote.

Since we are only partially present, lack of eye contact has become the norm in real life. Online we are apparently uncomfortable, so in its new iOS 13 update to FaceTime, Apple is experimenting with faking eye contact (or our "attention," in Apple's own jargon) and altering our faces so it looks like we are looking directly at the other person (Wilson, 2019).

If we can't see context, manners disappear, and ethical behavior deteriorates. The ease with which we can connect with people through social media, including strangers, has impaired our ability to communicate "IRL." The fact that there is an abbreviation like this one ("In Real Life") is, of course, itself very telling. IRL was the only place where we lived, once upon a time.

Location technologies, mobile and contextual sensors know everything about us: where we are, what the weather is like, where we are going, what we are looking for, and whom we are with. They can even anticipate what we are likely to do next. Thus, they take control of our life experiences, and we stop noticing what is right before us. We may occasionally look up from the screen, but this is because we were encouraged to do so by a stream of slot machine notifications, usually to find a place that knows we are there and wants our money. This, according to Foursquare, is like a friend that taps us on the shoulder when there is something he or she deems relevant to the moment, but contextual mobile services are not our friends. We know nothing about them, and they know everything about us.

Of course, I share the concerns of many regarding our loss of privacy or the financial motives of businesses when technology knows everything, from our geographic location to our purchasing habits, and even our stress levels. However, I worry about something even more disturbing. My point in this book is that the danger is not that the technology knows what we want, but that it knows what we may not even realize that we want for lack of context to recognize it. We love technology because it is our guide dog or cane, but it is our reliance on it that is making us blind.

Context blindness is the disease of our time. I do not claim that context blindness for all humans is the same as the medically diagnosed context blindness of children with Asperger's or autism. These issues stem from very different sources. Scientists have found genetics, certain pesticides, and other environmental factors to be suspected culprits in the proliferation of autism. According to the Centers for Disease Control (CDC, 2020), statistics show that the number of people with autism is on the rise—one in every 59 American children in 2019—and not solely as a result of an increase in diagnoses. These statistics raise some questions: are people with autism giving us a glimpse into the human condition in the near future? Some characteristics of *caetextia* as described by experts in autism do resemble those of the average technology-using human. Is it possible that technology-driven context blindness is itself partially responsible for the explosion of autism spectrum disorder diagnoses? Could this be a case of humans driving our own evolution with our technology?

COVID-19 has made these questions even more pressing. Despite Zoom fatigue and the fact that for some people on the autism spectrum, video chatting can be a struggle (as it can intensify sensory triggers such as loud noise and bright lights), the sudden shift to video calls has mostly had advantages for people who have neurological difficulties with face-to-face interactions or with people all talking at the same time. Remote meetings with frequent lags between speakers have been a godsend for people with autism, reducing the stress and anxiety that stems from their difficulty recognizing when it's their turn to speak in real-life conversations (Sklar, 2020).

The signs that people with autism may display early indications of the human condition in the future were there long before the pandemic. The descriptions of autistic behaviors very often speak of a child sitting expressionless, constantly spinning the wheel of a toy car, his eyes fixed. He pays no attention when his name is called, oblivious to the situation around him. It seems to me that if we replace the toy truck with a smartphone, this is quite an accurate description of a high percentage of the world population today. As Juan Enriquez argues, "autism isn't so much a vestige of the past as a glimpse of what's to come: the next evolutionary step in an increasingly data-choked world."

This book is an inquiry into and a lamentation about our context blindness. Contextual technology has put us on the doorstep of a new reality, a moment of a completely different class from other moments—a sea change. The transformation we are undergoing is so fundamental that it may be the beginning of a new stage of human evolution—I call it *Homo caetextus*.

References

Arendt, H. (1973). *The origins of totalitarianism*. San Diego, CA: Harvest.

Asurion Research (2019, November 29). Americans check their phones 96 times a day. https://www.asurion.com/about/press-releases/americans-check-their-phones-96-times-a-day/

Caetextia. (2009). *Context Blindness & Asperger's Traits*. https://www.caetextia.com/

Carr, N. G. (2010). *The shallows: What the Internet is doing to our brains*. New York: W.W. Norton.

Centers for Disease Control and Prevention. (2020, September 25). Data & statistics on autism spectrum disorder. https://www.cdc.gov/ncbddd/autism/data.html

Gessen, M. (December 13, 2016). The Putin paradigm. *NYR Daily*. https://www.nybooks.com/daily/2016/12/13/putin-paradigm-how-trump-will-rule/

Green, J., Petty, J., Staff, L., Bromley, P., & Jones, L. (2020). The implications of face masks for babies and families during the COVID-19 pandemic: A discussion paper. *Journal of Neonatal Nursing*, *27*(1), 21–25.

Keen, A. (2011). *The cult of the amateur: How blogs, MySpace, YouTube and the rest of today's user-generated media are killing our culture and economy*. London, UK: Hachette.

Knox, R. (September 20, 2010). The fading art of the physical exam. *NPR*. https://www.npr.org/templates/story/story.php?storyId=129931999

Mitchell, P. (2012). *Contagious metaphor*. London, UK: A&C Black.

Morin, A. (August 26, 2014). Is technology ruining our ability to read emotions? Study says yes. *Forbes*. https://www.forbes.com/sites/amymorin/2014/08/26/is-technology-ruining-our-ability-to-read-emotions-study-says-yes/?sh=2e10ca846a50

Nicas, J., & Wichter, Z. (March 14, 2019). A worry for some pilots: Their hands-on flying skills are lacking. *New York Times*. https://www.nytimes.com/2019/03/14/business/automated-planes.html

Postman, N. (1992). *Technopoly: The surrender of culture to technology*. New York: Alfred Knopf.

Sklar, J. (April 24, 2020). "Zoom fatigue" is taxing the brain. Here's why that happens. *National Geographic*. http://on.natgeo.com/3pQVODs

Sontag, S. (2001). *Illness as metaphor and AIDS and its metaphors*. New York: Macmillan.

Strate, L. (2006). *Echoes and reflections: On media ecology as a field of study*. Cresskill, NJ: Hampton Press.

Tessler, Y. (March 28, 2013). Haredi weekly censors female Holocaust victims. *Ynet*. https://www.ynetnews.com/articles/0,7340,L-4361353,00.html

Turkle, S. (2017). *Alone together: Why we expect more from technology and less from each other*. New York: Basic Books.

Wallace, B. (October 26, 2012). Autism spectrum: Are you on it? *New York Magazine*. https://nymag.com/news/features/autism-spectrum-2012-11/

Wilson, M. (July 3, 2019).Welcome to post-reality: Apple will now fake your eye contact in FaceTime. *Fast Company*. https://www.fastcompany.com/90372724/welcome-to-post-reality-apple-will-now-fake-your-eye-contact-in-facetime

Zaman, J. A. B. (2018). The enduring value of the physical examination. *Medical Clinics, 102*(3), 417–423.

PART I

CONTEXT BLINDNESS IN CONTEXT: SLOW ATROPHY

CHAPTER ONE

That Was Then; This Is Now: Media and Decontextualized Information

Scientific discoveries, as well as popular culture representations of Alzheimer's, have increased public awareness of the condition, as well as of the inherent plasticity of the brain. "Use it or lose it" is a commonly used phrase in the discourse around the deterioration of cognitive performance with aging, and a myriad of companies now offer "neuro-enhancing" games and puzzles. Evidence for the assertion that these games lower the risk of cognitive decline is lacking. Still, Christmas shopping lists now include presents such as *Sudoku for Seniors* and yearly subscriptions to *Lumosity*. We worry about our senior-future and neglect our present, willfully and happily delegating many of our brain's activities to digital technology.

We love our technology. It makes life better—smoother, cleaner, more comfortable, or more fun—but a more comfortable life comes with a price. When we delegate them to technology, our abilities slowly atrophy, and we end up losing them entirely. In Nicholas Carr's (2010) words, "…as we cede to software more of the toil of thinking, we are likely diminishing our own brainpower in subtle but meaningful ways" (p. 176).

In an article in the *New Yorker,* Tim Wu (2014) lists some of the tasks we are now unable to perform because technology performs them for us. He explains that "demanding" technologies such as a piano take time to master. Their usage is highly occupying, and their operation includes some real risk of failure. As opposed to these, "convenience" technologies such as instant cake-mixes promise "freedom from a life of drudgery and more space in our lives to focus on what we really care about," but they put us at a higher risk of biological atrophy.

Demanding technologies always require new learning. In the process of using them, the brain is stimulated and forced to change, but when things are too easy, as they increasingly are with convenience technologies, we neglect the biological need to be challenged and lose some of our abilities. When digital brain skills increase, human brain skills decrease as well until the unused capacities melt away entirely and we cannot run them autonomously.

Every medium of communication in history has weakened particular abilities. The delegation of our biological memory to writing long before digital media is an especially clear example. As Plato warned (speaking as Socrates relating the myth of king Thamus to Phaedrus): "those who acquire [writing] will cease to exercise their memory and become forgetful. They will rely on writing to bring things to their remembrance by external signs, instead of by their own internal remembrances" (in Postman, 1992, p. 4).

I had a chemistry teacher in middle school in Mexico where I grew up who did not allow us to take notes or copy anything off the blackboard. We found the rule weird and quite unnerving. It was, after all, chemistry and not, let's say, literature—equations and not stories. We protested, but to no avail. Apparently, he knew something about the effects of technology on humans. He understood, albeit intuitively, that when we take notes in class or copy from the board, we are postponing the remembering stage to a later date. The lecture goes from the teacher to the students' ears, their writing hands, and then their notebooks, bypassing the head, waiting for the final exam to go from the notebook or laptop to the eyes to the hand, and then to the test. Then to oblivion.

Not having written anything down then, I still know the periodic table by heart, in Spanish, 42 years later. Unless I am ever on *Who Wants to Be a Millionaire*, I don't have much use for it in my personal or professional life, but the fact that I know it serves as an illustration of one of the most central effects that writing had on humans: the deterioration of our memories.

Television too has weakened certain capabilities. With its emphasis on images, television has led to the deterioration of our verbal ability and the rational and coherent organization of ideas that words make possible. In turn, feelings and emotions have taken center stage, as they are what images evoke.

Based on this logic—that media take over specific skills, which we then end up losing—the thesis of this book is that digital media have damaged our ability to understand context. It is no coincidence that these latest technologies have come to be known as "contextual technologies."

Until about a decade ago, targeted ads were the main kind of contextual technology that most people experienced. They were invented in the mid-90s, and the technology would match ads to people by analyzing the search terms they used and the websites they repeatedly visited. The ads often offered irrelevant goods and services, but technology has evolved and now connects actual data acquired through sensors, mapping services, and social networks, providing users with personalized services that are more relevant to them. Moreover, technology now anticipates our needs and is "pro-active" at delivering solutions.

As data is now hosted on large clouds (storage systems), information is more accessible than ever, which facilitates integration of real-time data with contextual information. This is how our phones receive alerts to the fact that we are near a café that a Facebook friend of ours "liked" at noon, which is the time we usually have lunch.

Way beyond the targeted ads of the 90s, contextual technology now learns our preferences, monitors our surroundings, and alerts us to opportunities in them or in ourselves, like when wearable technologies such as watches alert us if our pulse is too high or if we are dangerously stressed. By understanding and reading context themselves, these technologies release us from the need to contextualize or to be aware of context.

The decontextualization of information did not start with digital technology. Our difficulty in reading context is the cumulative effect of the increasing decontextualization of information over the history of media. Aside from speech, where the participants in a conversation are present in the same place at the same time, every medium of communication has decontextualized information.

As a graduate student in the late 1980s, I was a teaching fellow and assistant to Neil Postman. He used to give a special lecture every year titled "How to give a speech." It was all about context. It included advice such as to try to visit the room where one's speech is to take place in advance, to familiarize oneself with the space, the props, the acoustics, etc. As opposed to the widespread belief these days that a written-out talk or a speech is a no-no, Postman advised writing out speeches and reading and re-reading them until we knew them by heart. He explained that this would ensure there would be no rambling, going off on tangents, exceeding the time limit allotted, and otherwise abusing one's audience. The most important qualification to this rule, however, was that the speech should be written for the ear and not for the eye, and he provided concrete techniques to achieve this.

The idea behind this advice is that the context of a speech is a live audience. In writing, the words are detached from their original context. The person is removed from the message. As Strate (2014) explains,

> In contrast to face-to-face communication, writing takes language out of a particular context of time and space, and in doing so, it gives our words a degree of permanence they would not otherwise obtain. [This comes] at the cost of not only the present as a situation involving immediate and direct communication but also the presence of a living breathing human being. (p. 15)

Writing renders language in an abstract and decontextualized form. The writer does not come into contact with the readers, and they are forced to recontextualize the message and interpret it, unable to ask the writer to elaborate or explain. As Christine Nystrom (1987) puts it: "What the alphabet did was separate thought from sensation, knowledge from experience, utterance from context, speech from speaker, and truth from presence, space, and time" (p. 112). Writing for the ear, then, is to connect with the listeners. They provide the context for the words spoken based on the words written.

Making lists is another example of the decontextualization of information by writing. Before writing, members of oral cultures used concepts in practical, everyday life situations with little abstraction. For instance, as Ong (1982) explains, asked to pick the one word that does not belong in the list "hammer, saw, log, hatchet," literate people choose "log," the only word that is not the name of a tool. Oral people, however, think situationally and see no use for tools if there is no log. A list of tools could not exist before writing, as "tools" is an abstract category not connected to any specific situation or human activity, like wood chopping or tree sawing. The list decontextualizes elements of speech; it detaches the items on the list from the contexts of human lives.

Jack Goody (1977) too, discusses the decontextualizing effect of lists specifically and of writing generally. He explains that lists impose boundaries—a beginning and an end—and that in oral situations, there are few if any occasions when one is required to list vegetables or trees, that applying techniques such as lists or tables to oral material results in the freezing of a contextual statement into a system of permanent oppositions, and that this comes at the expense of a real understanding of the actor's frame of reference or context. As he puts it: "… to shift frames of reference and regard such tables as models of the camshaft behind the jigsaw is to mistake metaphor for mechanism" (p. 73). Or, in terms of the field of general semantics (Korzybski, 1958), it is to mistake the map for the territory. The metaphor and the map are abstractions of the mechanism and the territory, and the latter are decontextualized by the former, leading to a change in consciousness.

Electronic media decontextualize information, too. As Postman (1986) explains, the idea of a kind of content called "the news of the day," for example, is the creation of the telegraph—the first medium to effectively sever the tie between the concept of communication and the concept of transportation—and amplified by additional electronic media such as radio and television. These media made it possible to transmit decontextualized information over immense spaces at an extraordinary speed, so we are constantly exposed to pieces of information from around the globe without any context, detached from their logical or habitual situation to help us make meaning of them, let alone act upon them (Strate, 2014). News on TV is never useful in our daily lives. We don't change our plans based on it, aside from perhaps the occasional weather or road-closing report. There is nothing we can do about Iran, North Korea, or Afghanistan. Our ongoing exposure to decontextualized information on television has taken a cumulative toll on our ability to understand context.

Some may suggest that literacy is more decontextualizing than television, and that television actually restores some sense of context. An argument can be made that the involvement of more senses in the consumption of television, which uses both video and audio (which are analogic and thus look and sound like the reality they capture), provides context in a way the symbol system of print (black scribbles on white pages) cannot. However, what we experience when watching television is an illusion of information in context. This illusion stems from the fact that we have gotten used to the language of film and television. Its "grammar" is so familiar to us by now that we forget that there is no such thing as a close-up in real life, for example, or that the transition from one place to another and from one time to another, made possible by editing, does not exist in the context of the reality presented—or rather re-presented.

Literacy, as previously mentioned, is quite decontextualizing. Still, print imposes a coherent arrangement of ideas and encourages a logically ordered public discourse. On television, we have grown accustomed to the decontextualized experience of watching programs about completely different subjects beginning every half-hour. We no longer expect what Neil Postman (1986) calls "consistency of tone" or "continuity of content" from television (p. 104).

As he was driving me home to Queens after class one evening, Postman told me a story. About two years earlier, he had had a meeting with a student who asked to see him during office hours to dispute her grade. She had brought her paper with her and wanted to discuss one of her professor's specific remarks. On page 7, Postman had written that her assumption there was the exact opposite of what the student had presented as her underlying assumption just a few paragraphs earlier. The student kept silent, as if waiting for Professor Postman to continue until the silence became uncomfortable, and she asked, "Yeah? So? What is the problem?" Postman tried to explain again, but the student stopped him and said: "But that was there, the top of the page, and this is here, mid-page."

"That was then; this is now," became the code-phrase to describe encounters with students in our department, many of which pointed to their difficulty to understand context. They struggled to grasp that one cannot present two conflicting theories as both underlying one's thesis within a single paper. Postman (1986) included the story in his book *Amusing Ourselves to Death*.

The "that was then; this is now" mode is present everywhere today. One example from the news in Israel in recent years is the Attorney General of Israel's recommendation on February 28, 2019, to prosecute Benjamin Netanyahu for bribery, fraud, and breach of trust. In spite of public calls for him to resign, Bibi did not do so, and he was re-elected. In 2008, which was the last time an Israeli prime minister was probed for corruption, then-opposition leader Netanyahu called on Ehud Olmert to resign. He warned that a leader "neck-deep in investigations has no moral mandate to make crucial decisions" (TOI Staff, 2018). So what? That was then; this is now.

Israel's education minister's remarks in the summer of 2019 are another example. He said in an interview that it is "possible" to perform gay conversion therapy, claiming that he had done so in the past. Faced by growing criticism, he called conversion therapy "inappropriate," and added that he was adamantly opposed to it. He said this was his unequivocal position (Kadari-Ovadia, 2019). This position was expressed just a few days after the original one, and his statement did not include an apology or an explanation for his change of mind. So what? That was then, and this is now.

"That was then; this is now" is the mode of thought of a public exposed for too long to television news and its use of "now…this." As Postman explains, "now…this" is a phrase used by news anchors on television, a conjunction that does not connect anything to anything but separates everything from everything. It indicates that what one has just heard or seen has no relevance to what one is about to hear or see. A news story is a discrete event, separated in content, context, and emotional texture from the one that came before it and the one following.

What made the "now…this" worldview even more problematic is that we stopped finding these discontinuities to be weird or unusual. The discourse of television that abandoned logic, reason, and sequence became the norm. We got used to it, stopped noticing the contradictions, and lost sight of any coherent or continuous context. When there is no context, contradictions disappear.

In *Within the Context of No Context,* George Trow (1997) blames television for damaging Americans' sense of history. He explains that the real contexts of citizens' lives (bowling clubs, for example), were replaced by the false contexts of television. "Television is the force of no-history," he writes, and its work is "to establish false contexts and to chronicle the unraveling of existing contexts; finally, to establish the context of no-context and to chronicle it" (p. 82).

The decontextualization of information has become even more substantial since Trow's and Postman's analyses. A May 2019 report by RAND (RAND, 2019), which focused on the linguistic analysis of newspapers, network and cable TV news, and online news, found that TV news has increasingly become more emotional, subjective, personal, and conversational, and the line between opinion and fact has been blurred accordingly. When context is lost, the first-person perspective flourishes on TV news, and there is more argument, dogma, and personal opinions. In online news platforms such as BuzzFeed, Politico, The Huffington Post, and Breitbart, key social and policy issues are narrated through very personal frames and subjective references.

Opinion and subjectivity are the characteristics of communication generally, and not only of journalism, in the digital age. "Alternative facts," a phrase that in other times would be regarded as an oxymoron, flourishes when opinion reigns, and there is no backdrop against which to judge reality. When there is no shared context, "whataboutism" abounds, and the "both sides" argument replaces rational debate. The "very fine people on both sides" in Charlottesville—demonstrators against white supremacy on one side, and neo-Nazis on the other—is an argument characteristic of the "context of no context" Trow and Postman warned about.

In the age of Twitter, the "then" and "now" in "that was then, this is now" are separated by no more than a few days at most. Donald Trump continually contradicted himself, going back and forth on gun control and background checks. He went from defending the separation of children from their parents to signing an executive order that stopped that policy within hours. He told Rex Tillerson that he was wasting his time trying to negotiate with "Little Rocket Man," and then visited North Korea. He flip-flopped around whether the United States would impose sanctions against Turkey over its purchase of a Russian S-400 air defense system. Inspired by these constant flip-flops, a man created flip-flops out of Trump's contradictory tweets, and he sold out his entire inventory in less than a month on his website (Morrison, n.d.). The slogan on the website is "going back on your word, one step at a time." There is a Syria edition, an electoral college edition, and a sources edition with the "very dishonest media" tweet on one foot and the one about the "very credible source" who told him Obama's birth certificate was a fraud on the other. The left foot was then, and the right foot is now. We don't remember the "then" and exist only in the "now," in the eternal present. As Douglas Rushkoff (2013) explains, our society has reoriented itself to the present moment. Everything is live, real-time, and always on. He illustrates:

> It's why the world's leading search engine is evolving into a live, customized, and predictive flow of data branded "Google Now"; why email is giving way to texting, and why blogs are being superseded by Twitter feeds… It's why kids in school can no longer follow linear arguments; why narrative structure collapsed into reality TV; and why we can't engage in meaningful dialogue about last month's books and music, much less long-term global issues… If the end of the twentieth century can be characterized by futurism, the twenty-first can be defined by presentism. (p. 23)

Meetup is also an example of presentism. It is a platform used to organize online groups that host in-person events that continually readjusts to its current context (Shirky, 2009). The question that Meetup poses to its members is, "What kind of group is a good idea right now?" Not in the current political atmosphere, not at the beginning of the third decade of the twenty-first century, but right now. The users' behavior guides the creation of new groups and the retiring of old ones and, since users live in a context-free present, without a temporal reference they are context-blind.

The weakening of our memory with the invention of writing, the shortening of our attention span due to television, and the deterioration of our social skills and manners with the increasing use of social media were all telltale signs of our impending context blindness.

Weakening of memory has become more marked, as we have delegated more if not all of our memory functions to Google. When we know we have access to the name of a celebrity that escapes us or to the definition of a word, we don't have to remember anything. As discovered in various studies (e.g., Sparrow et al., 2011), this results in lower rates of recall. It is why my students regularly ask me to repeat ideas verbatim, as if I were dictating instead of teaching. Instead of following ideas, understanding, and summarizing them in their own words, they want to type my exact words on their laptops, immediately forget them, and have them ready for access before their final exam.

Memory is impaired further by students' typewriting instead of handwriting. Various studies (e.g., Smoker et al., 2009) have shown that the use of paper and pen results in better memory due to the additional context provided by the complex task of writing. Very few students opt for writing, and quality penmanship has become a lost art. In their exams, arrows and hand-drawn emojis have replaced punctuation, except for multiple exclamation marks at the end of sentences. They are oblivious to the difference between the context of personal text messages and the academic context. In the former, we express feelings using smiley faces, all caps, or exclamation marks, while the latter requires a higher linguistic register and adherence to rules of grammar and punctuation.

Students also have a tough time concentrating for long periods. Early on in my teaching career in the late 80s and early 90s, I adopted a trick suggested to me by a colleague to finish a lecture successfully. When they began to move uncomfortably in their chairs or look at their watches, around an hour into class ("the great buttock shift," as we called it), I gave them one minute to stretch and yawn and be ready to listen again. I still use this method, but today they need the break around half an hour into class.

The shortening of our attention span began with television generally and with TV commercials specifically in that, as Christine Nystrom (1977) explains, they fixated us on the present and promised instant food, instant weight loss, and instant success. But attention spans have been compressed further due to the continuous shortening of texts on most digital platforms and the instant gratification that the Internet provides. The weight loss magic pills now arrive at our homes in just hours with Amazon Prime. We all have a harder time staying focused and paying attention.

Our social skills have suffered, too. I remember very vividly feeling deeply hurt by an experience I had when mobile phones were becoming popular. I was on my way to a meeting in Tel Aviv. I parked the car and started walking in the direction of what I thought was the address I needed. As it turned out, I was in the wrong area. Still excited about having found a parking spot in a city where finding a parking space is like winning a jackpot, I decided to walk and not move the car. I didn't know which direction to go. The neighborhood is an older part of town with small, quiet streets, and there was no one around to ask. It was getting late. Just as I was about to call to apologize, a woman turned the corner talking on her phone. Using every possible gesture to project politeness, I stopped her and beginning with the words "excuse me," I asked for directions. She stopped, said "hold on" to the person on the other side of the line, and with palpable anger said "No. I can't tell you how to get there. Can't you see I am on the phone?" and walked away.

It was not until much later that—as often happens to me—I thought of what I should have answered, screaming at her as she walked away: "If you stopped and put your phone away from your ear, why not use the 27 seconds of our encounter to help me rather than lecture me?" At that moment, however, all I could do was pull myself together, wipe away my tears of frustration, and look for another human being to ask. It was not until I used the story to illustrate a point in class that I could see the event for what it was: a sign of the changing definition of "public space." Our manners were starting to coarsen. It was the beginning of the final delegation of orientation in space to Waze or Google Maps, of the entrustment of human interaction to smartphones and social media. Now we can ignore everyone in the world, look at our phone, and act annoyed if the cashier at the supermarket (if there still is one) dares talk to us as she moves our groceries along. We can ignore everyone at the train station and not interrupt our games or tweets. We can walk and text, making it everyone else's responsibility to move out of our way and not bump into us.

The art of small talk is all but gone, too. Small talk requires attention to situations, eye contact to read the non-verbal cues of people around us, attention to context. We are busy making eye contact with ourselves for our selfies. We can't make eye contact because we are always looking at our phones. We don't know how to wait for someone at a coffee shop or look out the window during a cab ride. We are very uncomfortable without our props.

I almost miss the student who, nearly 30 years ago, came into my office, sat down wearing his earphones, listening to loud music on a Walkman. I could hear the headphones buzzing from the bass sounds. To my request to take them off, he answered: "I hear you just fine." At least he was looking at me.

References

Carr, N. G. (2010). *The shallows: What the Internet is doing to our brains.* New York: W.W. Norton.

Goody, J. (1977). *The domestication of the savage mind.* New York: Cambridge University Press.

Kadari-Ovadia, S. (July 16, 2019). Israel's Education Minister now says he opposes gay "Conversion Therapy". *Haaretz.* https://www.haaretz.com/israel-news/.premium-israel-s-education-minister-now-says-he-opposes-gay-conversion-therapy-1.7532713

Korzybski, A. (1958). *Science and sanity: An introduction to non-Aristotelian systems and general semantics.* Lakeville, CT: Institute of GS.

Morrison, S. (n.d.). *President Flip Flops.* https://www.presidentflipflops.com/

Nystrom, C. (1987). Literacy as deviance. *ETC: A Review of General Semantics, 44*(2), 111–115.

Nystrom, C. L. (1977). Immediate man: The symbolic environment of fanaticism. *ETC: A Review of General Semantics, 34*(1), 19–34.

Ong, W. J. (1982). *Orality and literacy: The technologizing of the word.* London: Methuen.

Postman, N. (1986). *Amusing ourselves to death: Public discourse in the age of show business.* New York: Penguin Books.

Postman, N. (1992). *Technopoly: The surrender of culture to technology.* New York: Alfred A. Knopf.

RAND Corporation Report. (2019). News in the Digital Age. https://www.rand.org/pubs/research_reports/RR2960.html

Rushkoff, D. (2013). *Present shock: When everything happens now.* New York: Current.

Shirkey, C. (2009). *Here comes everybody: The power of organizing without organizations.* New York: Penguin Books.

Smoker, T. J., Murphy, C. E., & Rockwell, A. K. (2009, October). Comparing memory for handwriting versus typing. In *Proceedings of the Human Factors and Ergonomics Society Annual Meeting* (Vol. 53, No. 22, pp. 1744–1747). Los Angeles, CA: SAGE Publications.

Sparrow, B., Liu, J., & Wegner, D. M. (2011). Google effects on memory: Cognitive consequences of having information at our fingertips. *Science, 333*(6043), 776–778.

Strate, L. (2014). *Amazing ourselves to death: Neil Postman's brave new world revisited.* New York: Peter Lang.

TOI Staff. (February 15, 2018). Zionist Union quotes Netanyahu in massive billboard urging him to quit. *Times of Israel.* https://www.timesofisrael.com/zionist-union-quotes-netanyahu-in-massive-billboard-urging-him-to-quit/

Trow, G. W. (1997). *Within the context of no context.* New York: Atlantic Monthly Press.

Wu, T. (February 21, 2014). The problem with easy technology. *The New Yorker*. https://www.newyorker.com/tech/annals-of-technology/the-problem-with-easy-technology

CHAPTER TWO

New Paradigms as Premature Symptoms: Emotional Intelligence and Soft Skills

Very significant changes in people's behavior started to become apparent sometime after the introduction of mobile phones and later, smartphones. In both private and public spaces, we experienced the sound pollution that came with the all-encompassing and constant phone rings and text notifications. The phones' blue lights lit up like fireflies in dark movie theaters, un-suspending our valuable suspension of disbelief and ruining the movie experience. New gestures were born, and tapping our jacket pockets or the back of our jeans, not sure if it was our phone that just rang or buzzed, became a common sight.

We started to walk and text. Apps were developed that used the phone camera as a screen-background. This allowed us to text and see stairs, crossings, and curbs on the street in the back of our texts (Zolfagharifard, 2014). Manners seemed to disappear, and smartphone use soon became grounds for divorce. All this, it was apparent, was an actual new phenomenon, all-encompassing and universal.

Various theories were offered to frame and explain the phenomenon. In hindsight, I believe these theories were cries for context. Two of the most widespread ideas to explain the deterioration of people's social behavior were "emotional intelligence" and "soft skills."

Soft skills are abilities such as good communication, organization, teamwork, planning, and time management, and they are called "soft" to distinguish them from "hard" skills, the job-specific abilities and knowledge necessary to perform a job successfully such as auditing for accountants, lesson planning for teachers, etc.

With the popularization of the term "soft skills," it became a new standard, and courses were crafted for millennials and Gen Z, the generations that seemed to be lacking in these skills the most. Some of the courses were initiatives of governments or the European Union that even financed them as a response to new problems that companies were facing. Employers began to notice characteristics of recently hired young people that they hadn't seen in previous generations of new employees.

My colleagues and I were planning to make changes to our advertising program of study. We interviewed the heads of some of the largest ad agencies in Israel, trying to find out what professional capabilities they were looking for in employees. Based on their answers, we would introduce new workshops to prepare our students for the world they would encounter after graduation.

What we came away with was a real revelation. All of our interviewees made one thing very clear: What the agencies needed from us were not graduates who were well versed in cinemagraphs, Facebook in-stream ads, TikTok or influencer marketing. These hard skills, they said, they could teach them over the first few months on the job. They were desperate for employees who got to work on time, who managed their time well, who were good at teamwork, and who wouldn't quit after a few months to search for better opportunities that would make them happier. The advertising executives wanted employees with excellent soft skills, affirming the saying that "hard skills will get you an interview, but it's soft skills that get you a job."

It is no wonder that a "millennial employee retention strategy" Google search now yields 27 pages of results. Soft skills are interpersonal competencies that did not require a title or a category up until not so long ago, since they were obvious. We grew up knowing they were necessary, and if they fell under a title at all, it was the characteristics of what my mother calls a "mensch."

Soft skills became scarce, so they began to be in demand. A Microsoft survey (Tims, 2011) found that business leaders rated soft skills above academic qualifications, and Google analyzed their teams for innovation and productivity and found that the seven top characteristics of success at their company were all soft skills (Agarwal, 2018). These included listening, having empathy toward colleagues, and being a good problem-solver. In Europe, colleges and universities are now obliged to include soft skills such as employability and lifelong learning in their curriculum. In 2016, I was myself asked to develop and teach a soft skills course for the National Professional Advancement Service of Paraguay.

The understanding of the need for these competencies was a paradigm shift from the long reign of hard skills. This paradigm shift happened because our understanding of the world clashed dramatically with our experience of the world, not just in the workplace, and not just for millennials. The clash is even more apparent today.

Take, for example, the dress code for parents at James Madison High School that prohibits parents from visiting the school wearing ripped jeans, leggings, shorts, mini-dresses, or tops that expose cleavage (Nittle, 2019). Hair bonnets, rollers, and pajama pants are banned as well. The critics of the dress code who claim it is racist and classist have a point. The high school serves mostly low-income families of color, and some of the items on the banned list disproportionately target black women's grooming practices. The backlash, based on accusations of respectability politics, is understandable. However, the school's decision to create the dress code can also be construed as resulting from eroding soft skills due to context blindness.

The context of a parent-teacher conference was once obviously different from the context of the home or of leisure. What one wore at home was different from what one wore in public. What girls wore was different from what was regarded as acceptable for women to wear, even in the absence of a dress code. In the digital age, however, the "adultified" child and the "childified" adult that Postman (1985) attributed to television have completely solidified as categories. When parents dress for a meeting with their children's teacher as they would dress to go to the beach, it is due to waning soft skills; so is the decision of school administrators to tackle the phenomenon with a dress code for parents. They are all blind to context because they are all living in their social media accounts. There, their photos in a bathing suit appear next to those of them wearing a business suit. They are equally clickable under "photos," and their appearance in their feeds or stories has no specific logic or rules. For administrators who are also living on Facebook, children and adults are all "friends."

Deficient soft skills are apparent not only in the United States; school dress codes seem to be an especially instructive area. A school in Israel recently forced a 7-year-old girl to spend the day in just her underwear and a T-shirt because she arrived on a particularly hot day in a sleeveless dress, contrary to school rules (Fox, 2020). The teacher refused to allow the girl to wear a sweater her mother had put in her bag in case it got cold in class because the sweater did not have the school emblem on it. Rather than hand her the T-shirt and ask her to wear it over the dress, the teacher insisted the girl wear the T-shirt in place of the dress.

Apparently based on some misguided conception of modesty, sleeveless dresses are not allowed at school. T-shirts on top of mere underwear apparently are allowed, regardless of the humiliation and suffering of a small child. It is hard to decide what is at the basis of this story: idiocy, cruelty, or context blindness.

The paradigm-shift from IQ to EQ (emotional intelligence) in public discourse is closely related to the rise of the concept of soft skills. This shift was also a sign of the context blindness that would soon ensue. Many soft skills have a foundation in emotional intelligence, or the ability to understand and manage one's emotions—to identify, experience, and express feelings in healthy and productive ways.

With the paradigm shift it became popular to criticize the reductive nature of intelligence testing and the basic idea of multiple intelligences became accepted, as was the understanding that both academic intelligences, and more fluid intelligences and other factors such as interests and personality, are all important to academic, work, and life performances.

The theory of multiple intelligences was developed by Howard Gardner, a Professor of education at Harvard University, and he proposed eight different intelligences to account for a broader range of human potential in children and adults.

Motivated by the drive to explain a complicated reality (as I am in this book), Daniel Goleman (1995) proposed a broader view of intelligence than the one many subscribed to until his book, treating IQ as genetic and not modifiable by life experiences.

Goleman's book made it to the cover of Time Magazine in the US, became an international best-seller and Goleman became an "academic celebrity," appearing on TV shows such as Oprah Winfrey.

That narrow view of IQ, he says, does not explain what factors are at play in situations where people with a high IQ struggle while those with an average IQ succeed. He explains that our passions, when well exercised, have wisdom; they guide our thinking, our values, and our survival. The problem is not that one is emotional, but whether the emotion and its expression are appropriate. In other words, the problem is one of context, of the ability to understand context and decide what the proper emotions are in response to that context. Context sensitivity is the cornerstone of emotional intelligence, and it is a sensitivity we progressively lack. We are context-blind.

References

Agarwal, A. (October 2, 2018). Data reveals why the 'soft' in 'soft skills' is a major misnomer. *Forbes*. https://www.forbes.com/sites/anantagarwal/2018/10/02/data-reveals-why-the-soft-in-soft-skills-is-a-major-misnomer/?sh=2d75e5466f7b

Fox, N. (May 19, 2020). School forces 7-year-old girl to spend day in underwear for breaking dress code. *Ynet*. https://www.ynetnews.com/article/HkT45nWjL

Goleman, D. (1995). *Emotional intelligence: Why it can matter more than IQ*. New York: Bantam Books.

Nittle, N. (May 7, 2019). A high school's dress code for parents sparked backlash. The principal is standing by it. *Vox*. https://www.vox.com/the-goods/2019/5/7/18532416/james-madison-high-school-dress-code

Postman, N. (1985). The disappearance of childhood. *Childhood Education*, *61*(4), 286–293.

Tims, A. (March 5, 2011). The secret to understanding soft skills. *Guardian*. https://www.theguardian.com/money/2011/mar/05/secret-to-understanding-soft-skills

Zolfagharifard, E. (March 4, 2014). Text AND walk: App makes your mobile "transparent" so you can see the street in front of you while typing. *Daily Mail*. https://www.dailymail.co.uk/sciencetech/article-2573087/Text-AND-walk-App-makes-mobile-transparent-street-typing.html

CHAPTER THREE

Diagnosis: Caetextia—The Age of Autism

Something has gone terribly wrong over the past few years. The year 2020 alone was enough to make one's head spin: Fake news about the source of the coronavirus (the Chinese, a laboratory, bats, pangolins), mismanagement of the pandemic (by the leaders of multiple countries, including those of the U.S., Mexico, and Brazil), the politicization of face masks, the conspiracy theories that culminated in the attack on the Capitol building in the United States in January 2021, police brutality, and demonstrations throughout the world, to mention only a few. All these have made it hard to find coherence and to make meaning of what is happening. It has become harder than ever to know what's true and what's not, to find order or logic in events everywhere in the world. Life feels random, irrational, and capricious.

Sometimes it seems like we are getting used to this kind of absurd existence. It is too tiring to try to make sense of things all the time. We become accustomed to and normalize the absurd. It is hard not to, as humans yearn for normal, but the drive to explain how we got here is strong, and it has led me to the idea of context blindness.

I use the term "context blindness" as a metaphor for the human condition in this technological age—but, as it turns out, it may not be entirely metaphorical. Context blindness, or *caetextia* in Latin, is a term coined by Joe Griffin and Ivan Tyrrell in 2007 to describe the most dominant manifestation of autistic behavior at the highest levels of the autistic spectrum (Caetextia, 2009a). As I pointed out in the Introduction, the use of "autism" is by no means meant as a slur. In a story in *Time* magazine about trolls online, Joel Stein (2016) wrote, "Now the web is a sociopath with Asperger's." The sentence drew a lot of criticism. It was removed, and an editor's note of apology was added to the online version, but the apology hardly appeased Max Sparrow (Unstrange Mind, 2016), an autistic author and advocate who in an open letter to *Time* wrote:

> I am autistic. In your article published online this morning, you engage in the behavior you purport to bemoan. You have trolled me on the Internet…Did you not realize that you were crafting words of hate that are massively damaging to a population that already suffers hate and abuse? Did it not occur to you that your words would feed the depression of countless autistics — myself among them — who grapple with depression, anxiety, PTSD, and a pervasive feeling that we live in a world that would rather see us dead than help us have quality of life?... If you truly care about a culture of hate on the Internet, you will retract your hate speech. You will apologize to autistics and people with Asperger's…and you will never again deem it appropriate to use a vulnerable disabled population to make a pithy point. We are not your linguistic color; we are human beings. (n.p.)

I do not use autism for linguistic color in this book. My point is rather that autistics' difficulty in imagining minds other than their own and their struggle with social skills may be a preview of our imminent context-blind human circumstances.

Why does the moon look bigger on the horizon? Why can we tell the difference between a sincere and a polite smile? Why do we recognize words before they are fully spoken out? The answer is that we are sensitive to context. Nothing that we perceive has an absolute meaning. Tears can mean sadness, but also happiness, relief, or the result of making onion soup. When you are in the middle of a crosswalk, a red light no longer means "stop," but "hurry up."

Peter Vermeulen, one of the leading proponents of autism as context blindness, uses these questions to illustrate the influence of context on the meaning of what we perceive. Context, he explains (2011), helps us focus on what is relevant and to ignore what is irrelevant. It helps us make sense of vague, incomplete, or ambiguous information. We use context to understand the behaviors and the minds of others and to make sense of the world, to make it predictable. People with autism, on the other hand, lack a spontaneous use of context when giving meaning, especially to vague and ambiguous stimuli.

Autism is regarded as a spectrum disorder, a continuum between serious cases and milder ones; it is also a syndrome, which means that it includes a large range of characteristics that may or may not appear in different cases and in various combinations.

The main areas of difficulty for autistics are social interaction (problems developing relationships, reciprocating emotions, blindness to non-verbal social cues, deficiency in verbal and non-verbal communication, and restricted and repetitive patterns of behavior).

Since Leo Kanner (1943) published the first systematic description of early infantile autism in 1943, the quest for an explanation of autism resulted in three major hypotheses: weak central coherence, executive dysfunction, and Theory of Mind.

The theory of weak central coherence asserts that people with autism have difficulties in seeing "the big picture." The theory of executive dysfunction postulates that autism is the result of deficits in flexibility, planning, and other high-cognitive functions for organizing and controlling reactions.

According to the Theory of Mind, autistics have trouble mind reading or attributing mental states (feelings, wishes, knowledge, intentions) to themselves and others. They are afflicted by "mind-blindness" (Baron-Cohen, 1997). They cannot, like neurotypical people, mind-read automatically and without effort and participate in social relations and communications. To make sense of actions, to predict, and interpret looks requires decoding "the language of the eyes" (Baron-Cohen et al., 1997). To these, a theory has been added that people with autism are good at understanding events organized and caused by rules and systems (systemizing) but are less successful at understanding events caused by human agents (empathizing) (Wheelwright & Baron-Cohen, 2011).

According to Vermeulen (2012), although these theories have considerably improved our understanding of autism, none of them succeeds in explaining the whole picture. In other words, none of them can reasonably account for all the behavioral characteristics of autism. For example, Theory of Mind explains social and communication difficulties, but it is hard to find a reasonable connection between the lack of Theory of Mind and rigid behaviors or resistance to change. He suggests that context is the key to understanding the condition, as all these theories have a diminished contextual sensitivity in common.

Vermeulen believes that the role of context is crucial in exactly those areas that are known to be affected by autism: social interaction, communication, and flexibility in thoughts and behavior. He explains:

> A good sense of context contributes significantly to our adaptability and our survival skills in a world without fixed meanings...Contextual sensitivity is vital for understanding other people's minds and behavior. Taking context into account is crucial for distinguishing what is relevant from what is circumstantial. A lack of contextual sensitivity results in misunderstanding the meaning not only of human behavior, but also of many events and even objects...The behavior and reactions of people with autism

> are mostly logical, but often at the same time seemingly a little inappropriate because they are out of context. (p. 19)

Contextual sensitivity helps us untangle the inherent ambiguity of stimuli and respond appropriately to them. When we lack contextual sensitivity, our spontaneous use of context when giving meaning to a stimulus is reduced. This reduced contextual sensitivity and flexibility is what is meant in this book by context blindness.

Strate (2006) explains:

> Language use for the autistic child may be so concrete, that a word learned with a particular individual, in a particular place, and during a particular activity, may not be generalized to other people, places, or situations... The self and world that autistics tend to construct is concrete to an extreme. In other words, they tend not to use abstract, global categories in their thought and perception, instead focusing on the particular, on concrete details. (p. 116)

The extreme awareness of a specific context described here may seem like the opposite of context blindness. However, as Strate himself adds, the extreme concreteness associated with autism is closely connected to trouble with language acquisition and language's concomitant capacity for abstraction. In other words, autistics have difficulty abstracting or generalizing. It is not that they cannot see or are blind to specific contexts, but rather that they don't have a sense of context. They may see a specific situation perfectly, but not notice in what ways that context or situation is similar to previous ones they have encountered—that the words and skills used there may be helpful in the new context, and that the behavior learned there fits here too. The world that autistics create is extremely specific. They do not use conceptual, comprehensive classifications, but instead they focus on specific, concrete details. As Vermeulen (2015) put it, "they do not use the forest to see the trees as trees" (p. 2).

Strate (2006) himself settled the seeming contradiction in his discussion of the oral and the literate elements in autism. He says:

> Autistics are naturally capable of a kind of detachment and objectivity that has for long been an ideal of Western literate cultures. Along the same lines, autistics tend to ignore context in their communication and behavior, whereas the act of writing by its very nature takes language out of its context of sound and accompanying nonverbal cues and out of the context of social interaction, place, and time...Literate decontextualization is often associated with abstraction (to abstract is to take something out of a more specific and detailed context), but the experience of autistics shows that it may also involve the removal of an abstract context, leaving behind nothing but the most concrete of elements. (p. 125)

The thesis in this book is that like autistics, we increasingly lead our daily lives paying attention to the most concrete elements before us, blind to the abstract context we have delegated to contextual digital technologies. Like people with autism, we are all progressively less able to use context spontaneously when giving meaning to real-life situations outside of our screens.

I arrived at this thesis at a point in time when the world felt like it had stopped making sense to me. It started about a decade ago with palpable changes in my students' knowledge. For a while, the talk among my colleagues was that students don't read and can't write, and that high school doesn't teach them what it used to—and that we can no longer assume that they possess knowledge of basic grammar, evolution, or the idea of democracy. To survive my job and regain some of my love for going to work, I decided to stop mourning and use every opportunity I had to enlighten them. Instead of showing them how shocked I was that they had never heard of Don Quixote, I stopped the class and gave a short lecture about Cervantes and the symbolism of "tilting at windmills."

This worked, but only for a while. Soon, my feeling was that new generations of students were not only less knowledgeable of the basics of the cultural canon; it was as if they were a different species from students a year or two earlier. They understood their roles as students differently. It was clear that higher education now played a different role in their lives. They were increasingly different from previous classes in their behavior and in what felt like an utter lack of manners. They had complete disregard for my time. They stopped me during breaks in the corridors of our building to ask questions our chance encounter seemed to have reminded them they wanted to ask. They had not handed in their assignments, they had missed class multiple times, or they had not studied for the quiz. Their questions couldn't wait for my office hours because they were worried about their grades.

This new brand of students was also much more sensitive. They were easily offended and cried a lot. Their emails amazed and confused me. For a while, I applied yet another resolution to my communication with them. Instead of getting mad at what seemed like chutzpah on their part, I decided to use the opportunity to educate them by politely pointing out why their tone of voice was inappropriate. I explained, for example, why handing a paper in late and writing, "I expect your prompt reply," was a problem. Their replies almost always included an apology and a clarification. They had had no intention of being disrespectful and, in fact, I had insulted them.

Books and academic papers started focusing on the differences between the past few generations, my own, my kids', and my students'. The literature about Generations X, Y, millennials, and Z provided some relief to my confusion. I felt like, if nothing else, at least I was not alone. It was not just me. Professors throughout the world were having some of the same experiences I was having. The explanation that it was the Internet, screens and screen-time, and the difference between immigrants and natives of the digital world made some sense.

I was settling into my new professorial persona. I was trying to find the appropriate rationalizations to ease the cognitive dissonance that came with giving in to the needs of my millennial students. I was also trying to find a way to function in spite of the mission of my college, which included the explicit definition of our students as customers. The feeling that my job as a professor didn't make sense anymore spread to most other areas of my life.

Donald Trump was elected President of the United States in 2016, and a general and constant feeling of amazement and disbelief has permeated every single day of my life ever since. There are no resolutions I can come up with and apply to ease my confusion. COVID-19, or rather the responses to the pandemic—aside from in a few countries such as New Zealand—have made things even worse.

What humans lack is contextual sensitivity. It seems we have lost the ability to discover contextually relevant information and ignore contextually unimportant information—the ability to select elements that are useful and meaningful and use them. This is manifested, as it is in people with autism, in our social interactions, communication, and flexibility (or lack thereof) in thoughts and behavior.

Humans rarely see faces out of context in real life. When we try to figure out what a person feels, we look at context as much as facial expressions. We look at the situation, what that person says, their body language, our past experiences with similar situations, etc. (Vermeulen, 2011). Based on all these, we recognize emotions. People with autism have difficulty with this, but increasingly, so do the rest of us due to the prevalence of our online interactions.

In "Empathy in the Digital Age," Daniel Goleman (2018) explains that in face-to-face interactions, our emotional centers operate quickly and unconsciously. They take in large amounts of information from the other person and send out impulses for how to respond. Meanwhile, other parts of our brains help guide those interactions by inhibiting emotional impulses that might drive the interaction in a bad direction.

Online interactions lack this feedback loop and the cues for emotional empathy, and we pick up little or none of what the other person actually feels, reacting mainly to what they write or text. From the emotional perspective, Goleman says, "we are flying blind—or numb." He adds:

> In brain terms, we get no inhibition of impulse from the prefrontal circuitry—thus "cyber-disinhibition." When we don't make the effort online to understand the other person's perspective, or how a given response might make them feel, the social distance

> of the Internet can quickly turn our worst impulses into words and deeds we would never think of in person, like leaking intimate photos and other forms of virtual harassment. (n.p.)

Vermeulen and others such as Uta Frith and Simon Baron-Cohen also propose that people with autism have difficulty controlling their emotions. They cannot detach from a conditioned response pattern to try to see the possible consequences of that response or consider other more beneficial ways of reacting. Thus, they feel confused and out of control, suffer extreme anxiety and anger, and can swing between wild mania and deep depression. When heavily stressed, they explain, "we can all become temporarily caetextic: prone to black-and-white, crazy, irrational behavior and faulty reasoning" (Caetextia, 2009b).

We are all indeed a bit caetextic (and not temporarily) as life in the digital age is inherently erratic and stressful. Tweets are pushed to our phones dozens of times a day and expose us to outrageous utterances. These are reacted-to and re-tweeted, repeated and inflated by news sources, each of which pulls us in different directions until we completely lose sight of any logical context. Like people with Asperger syndrome, we end up accepting absurdities as real and making judgments about them without the background information to apply to the context in which we find ourselves (Griffin & Tyrrell, 2008). Like them, we suffer from an absence of flexibility in behavior. Our behavior online is repetitive, and there is a rigidity in our reactions to the world.

My drive to explain life in the digital age has led me down the path of illness. My explanation is a bleak one: we are afflicted by a syndrome. We are ill. This explanation makes the world more intelligible and clear. It is the kind of clarity that comes with a long-expected diagnosis. We began to lose sight of context with writing, and we are now afflicted with full-blown blindness because we have entrusted context to the contextual technologies of the digital age. These technologies are the topic of Part II.

References

Baron-Cohen, S. (1997). *Mindblindness: An essay on autism and theory of mind.* Boston: MIT Press.

Baron-Cohen, S., Wheelwright, S., & Jolliffe, T. (1997). "Is there a" language of the eyes"? Evidence from normal adults, and adults with autism or Asperger syndrome." *Visual Cognition, 4*(3), 311–331.

Caetextia. (2009a). *Context Blindness & Asperger's Traits.* https://www.caetextia.com/

Caetextia. (2009b). *Left and Right Brain.* https://www.caetextia.com/pages/leftright.html

Goleman, D. (October 15, 2018). Empathy in the digital age. *Korn Ferry Institute.* https://www.kornferry.com/insights/this-week-in-leadership/emotional-intelligence-empathy-digital-age

Griffin, J., & Tyrrell, I. (2008). Parallel processing. *Human Givens Journal, 15*(4), 11–17.

Kanner, L. (1943). Autistic disturbances of affective contact. *Nervous Child, 2*(3), 217–250.

Stein, J. (August 18, 2016). How trolls are ruining the Internet. *TIME.* https://time.com/4457110/internet-trolls/

Strate, L. (2006). *Echoes and reflections: On media ecology as a field of study.* Cresskill, NJ: Hampton Press.

Unstrange Mind. (August 18, 2016). An open letter to Time Magazine and Joel Stein. http://unstrangemind.com/an-open-letter-to-time-magazine-and-joel-stein/

Vermeulen, P. (2011). Autism: From mind blindness to context blindness. *Asperger's Digest,* November/December.

Vermeulen, Peter. (2012). *Autism as context blindness.* Shawnee, KS: AAPC Publishing.

Vermeulen, P. (2015). Context blindness in autism spectrum disorder: Not using the forest to see the trees as trees. *Focus on Autism and Other Developmental Disabilities, 30*(3), 182–192.

Wheelwright, S., & Baron-Cohen, S. (2011). Systemizing and empathizing. In D. Fein (Ed.), *The Neuropsychology of Autism* (pp. 317–338). New York: Oxford.

PART II

CONTEXTUAL TECHNOLOGY, CONTEXT-BLIND USERS

CHAPTER FOUR

The Power of Context and the Importance of Situations

What is a nice birthday present for a good friend? What do you do when the bell rings? What do you put in your suitcase when you go traveling? No doubt you can answer each of these questions. But what if you were asked to give the one and only correct answer? You would probably reply, "It all depends..." A nice birthday present for one of your friends could be quite inappropriate for another. The bell may be a signal to remove the cake from the oven, go to your next class, or exit a building because of fire. What you pack in your suitcase depends on the destination and length of your journey. A "correct" answer for all of these questions depends on the situation, and another word for situation is context. (Vermeulen, 2011, n.p.)

Raising children makes us particularly aware of context—of situations. My awareness spiked one morning when driving my son to kindergarten. Traffic was heavy on the one street leading out of our neighborhood. Apparently very late for work, a father driving his daughter to school cut through the line of cars without blinking. I was startled, and I honked. As if out of the blue, I heard my four-year-old's voice from the back seat: "Mom, what is a son of a b...?" I wasn't sure I heard him right and asked, "What did you say, honey?" I had heard right.

I had just honked without saying a thing, so this was not a question about something I had just muttered. It was quite clear that my son associated the situation—our car, the traffic around us, the time of day, and the honking—with those specific words. I had probably used them in his presence more than once. I blushed for a brief moment, doubted if I was fit to be a mother, and then used the 6 minutes it took to get to kindergarten for his first lesson about context—about why some words are ok in one place and not in another. I am happy to announce 24 years later: he turned out to be a well-adjusted adult who uses profane language only in appropriate contexts.

Another question we face as parents is at what age it is ok to let a child cross a street alone. Most of the time, we intuitively know whether or not they are ready. We know, for example, that it is not enough that we have explained to them a thousand times that they need to wait for the light to change to green, look left and right to see that no cars are coming, and only then to cross. We are aware of how many things could go wrong, how much is unexpected, how important it is for them to be able to read a situation and use discretion. To use discretion means to be sensitive to context.

It is this sensitivity to context that as adults makes us comfortable when disobeying the law and crossing a deserted street in the middle of the night on a red light. We seem silly in our own eyes if we don't. In fact, even though there is no definitive research, what the available evidence strongly suggests is that pedestrians put themselves in danger if they wait for a walk signal instead of crossing the street whenever and wherever it looks safest (Ross, 2016). The basic idea that jaywalking is inherently unsafe is not supported by (indirect) statistical evidence. For example, data collected for New York's Vision Zero program (Vision Zero Action Plan, 2014) points to the fact that most pedestrian deaths and an even greater majority of non-fatal crashes occur while crossing the street lawfully in a crosswalk. Reading situations and understanding context saves lives. But what are situations? And what does it mean "to read" them?

According to Goffman (1959) situations are systems of communication, languages with their own grammar or rules for action. These communication systems, whether in a classroom, the beach, a movie theater, or a courtroom, structure our behavior and thought processes differently. Based on Goffman's theatrical metaphor, each of these is a different play where people act out different roles and maintain different limits or barriers between "the front and back regions," or the stage and the backstage. Each of these involves different locations, props, languages, and costumes; they lead to different performances and personal demeanors; they bring out of people different selves.

As Christine Nystrom (2021) explains:

> We do not recognize situations by their labels, locations of functions…We know where we are, I think, because we recognize-without even being aware that we are

> doing so—a set of conditions: conditions involving space; conditions involving time; conditions involving objects, symbols, and the transactions between people. And it matters because those conditions allow us not only to label a situation, but to predict how others will behave and what expectations they will have of us. In a sense, knowing where we are tells us who we are, and who are the others around us. (p. 60)

She explains further that the structure of the situation and not the content shapes the interaction among participants in that situation. She says:

> ...Content takes on specific meaning—that is, determines a particular set of responses and predictions—only within the structure of a given situation. What you make of "Please open the window" depends on where you are: addressed to you by the instructor in a classroom where all have equal access to the windows, it means one thing; by a stranger in a closed elevator, another thing; by a shabbily dressed man outside your car as you wait for the light, something else entirely...A smile, a touch on the arm, a wink of the eye—what do they mean? Outside of a specific context, a structured situation, it is impossible to say. In this sense, the "content" of messages is always subordinate, in human meaning-making, to the structure of situations. This is what Stanley Milgram means when he says, in another context, that "relationship overwhelms content"; what Erving Goffman means when he writes, of human communication, that its first priority is "to establish and maintain the definition of the situation"; what Marshall McLuhan means when he says "The medium is the message." (p. 68)

Situations are human environments that are "what Malinowski originally termed situational context...a product of social as well as biological and physical factors..." (Strate, 2017, p. 103). A classroom with desks and chairs organized in rows, with students facing the whiteboard and the backs of each other's heads, leads to a more formal interaction than a workshop-type classroom, with small groups of students gathered around small tables, spread out around the room. Even a small change or addition to the factors that make up the situation leads to a different interaction. Suppose we add balloons floating on the ceiling of the traditional classroom. In that case, we get a different interaction in terms of thoughts, feelings, and behaviors that fits the context of a birthday party at school.

Reading situations and sensitivity to context helps us interpret each other's words, actions, and emotions. Where we are, who we are with, and the things around us influence how we feel and act. Context shapes who we are and our role in the specific situation, but what happens to our roles, our selves, when so much of our daily lives now take place online?

Scholars have applied Goffman's ideas to the analysis of identity and presentation of the self online. Highlighting Goffman's front and backstage notion, some of these scholars (Bullinham & Vasconcelos, 2013) have proposed that online environments provide users the potential to perform and present different identities. They explain that in a mediated interaction, the physical distance of the actor from the audience facilitates the hiding of aspects of the offline self and the embellishment of the online self. They add that the online environment may be seen as a stage where we create and edit our onstage personae, and our lives offline as the backstage. However, the coronavirus pandemic may have revealed otherwise: that we are contextually insensitive, and that the backstage has leaked onto the stage.

Online activities have multiplied with COVID-19, raising multiple questions about reading situations and understanding context. I remember how amazed and incredulous I felt during the first few weeks of remote teaching and faculty meetings through Zoom at what seemed to me to be misread situations by students and even some of my colleagues. For example, whereas in a physical conference room we naturally and inevitably see each other from various angles when sitting around a table, all we can see on Zoom is each other's medium shot. This fact did not deter a colleague from "participating" in a committee meeting while simultaneously conducting an unrelated meeting at his real-world office. His microphone was off, and his phone camera was placed to his side, showing his low-angle profile as he faced his desktop. I have known this colleague as a pleasant and well-mannered professor for many years, but he was blind to the new context and insensitive to the lack of interest in his co-workers that he projected. He was politely asked by the Dean through private chat to turn off his camera. A black square somehow felt less insulting.

Many professors experienced a screen filled with black boxes with names in them for months teaching remotely. The question of whether it should be mandatory for students to open their cameras became the subject of heated debates at colleges and universities everywhere. On the one hand, there is the question of privacy and the intrusion into students' homes, as well as the understanding that students may have competing obligations, and not all of them have the circumstances at home (such as their own room and requisite technology) to allow them to turn on their cameras. On the other hand, there is the weird and unsettling experience of professors talking to black squares without any visual feedback to know, as we know from gestures and micro-cues in a physical classroom, whether someone seems confused or something needs to be repeated. To this, one can add the closed microphones, the limited audio feedback, the unnatural pauses, the need to monitor participation and amplify one person at a time, and the artificial silence that requires some getting used to.

Remote teaching is an entirely different situation from teaching in person in a classroom. It is a new context that revealed how contextually insensitive many of us are. We know how hard it is to spend hours and concentrate in front of a computer. There is even a term for it now: "Zoom fatigue." Granted, it can be difficult to prime ourselves psychologically for work or school-related interactions from home. We are not used to interacting formally at home. Students hold themselves respectfully or professionally in class, whereas at home, the environment (the elements of the situation, in Goffman's terms) sends us mixed messages as to what is proper. The situation of a class is a formal one, but at home we are too comfortable. Still, to "attend" class with a camera on, lying in bed under the covers, is to be context-blind.

In a piece published on the first day of school, Lance Strate (2020) described some of the incredible things taking place in the U.S. at the time. Students were being sent back to school with COVID-19 far from being under control. We somehow believed, he says, that classrooms and dorms would be safe for face-to-face learning. We thought that young children would be immune to the disease and not bring it home to their families, and that teenagers would wear masks and socially distance against their nature, that economic activity would just naturally resume.

Strate explains these beliefs, along with our confidence in our power to deal with climate change (even if it is probably too late), or our ability to cut taxes and maintain social security, based on Daniel Boorstin's idea that we are ruled by extravagant expectations rooted in false realities we have manufactured through media, technology, advertising, and PR, and that we are living in a constant state of denial of reality.

Towards the end of his article, Strate laments:

> Our nation needs leadership rooted in reality, not fantasy and wish-fulfillment. Tragically, we have a president who is a celebrity, not a leader. He gained that position through no achievement or qualification other than a knack for publicity, and a persona manufactured with the help of Mark Burnett, producer of *The Apprentice*. Boorstin defined the celebrity as "a person who is known for his well-knownness," someone "fabricated on purpose to satisfy our exaggerated expectations of human greatness," someone who represents "a new category of human emptiness." (n.p.)

Indeed, Donald Trump got to be president through *The Apprentice*, but once he became president, he lived on Twitter. Perhaps it was television—the medium at the center of Boorstin's thesis (1985)—that initially lead to extravagant expectations and denial of reality. However, it seems that digital technology and social networks have made our expectations even more extravagant because we are now one stage further from denial of reality. We are blind to reality, blind to context.

As Postman (1986) explains, the problem is not that television amuses. Amusement is good, but not in every context. It is one thing to fire apprentices on reality television, but in the context of the presidency, you end up with a record number of dismissals and resignations after record-short tenures (Michael Flynn, Reince Priebus, Anthony Scaramucci, and Tom Price, to name a few). It is one thing to think of striking deals as an art in business. In the context of international diplomacy, it manifests itself in a visit to North Korea to "make a deal" with "Little Rocket Man" and withdrawal from the Paris Agreement, claiming it undermines the U.S. economy and puts the U.S. at a permanent disadvantage. All this is even more dangerous because it is all conducted through Twitter.

"Twitter diplomacy" is dangerous because complex and nuanced policies cannot really be squeezed into tweets of 280 characters or less. Messages transmitted over Twitter at times of intense international tension result in dynamics different from those that have characterized communication through TV. Tweets reach global and diverse audiences. A tweet by the United States president, intended for his base, often contained hostile foreign policy elements that also reached foreign leaders. Trump's combative tone with all-caps and plenty of exclamation points made the tweets even more incendiary. His multiple tweets a day, unfiltered and unswayed by expert advice, reached tens of millions of followers domestically and internationally, including in Iran.

Trump was like Jerzy Kosinski's Chance in *Being There*, whose understanding of reality was shaped by television. Unlike Chance, however, Trump was viciously conscious of his actions and understood how to use this reality to his own advantage. The tool he used was Twitter. He loved it because it amplified the extreme political rhetoric he enjoyed promoting. It is what the algorithm is set to do. Tweets from people holding fringe views, containing heated political rhetoric, and advancing conspiracy theories and flat-out lies expose users to dangerous content, resulting in their radicalization.

Just as Postman (1986) says about TV—that the problem is not what people watch but that they watch—so it is with Tweeter. The content of Trump's tweets is almost irrelevant, "despite the constant negative press covfefe." It is the fact that he tweeted (until banned from the platform) that was itself problematic. He did it repeatedly in every situation, and with complete disregard for context.

The connection Lance Strate (2006, 2017) makes between McLuhan's concept of hot and cool media and Edward Hall's concept of high and low context cultures is very useful for understanding the folly of Trump's Twitter presidency and Twitter culture generally. According to Hall, in high-context cultures, less is communicated by the source, and more is expected of the receiver in terms of prior knowledge. In low-context cultures, the source tends to spell everything out, and the receiver is not expected to have prior knowledge to understand messages. In McLuhan's terms, low-context cultures can be characterized as hot media—a communication style in which the context for understanding the message is provided in the message. High-context cultures can be characterized as cool media—a communication style in which the participants assume that everyone has the information necessary to make sense of the message and that no explanation is needed. Twitter is a medium that does not provide context within the message; there is barely enough room for the message itself in 280 characters. However, the assumption that people have the information necessary to make sense of the message is misguided. It is a cool medium in a low-context culture, an environment where trolls flourish. When we don't share a context and our media don't provide it, we are easily distracted. It is easy to upset us and incite emotional reactions with provocative messages, digressions, and unrelated messages.

As Hall (1976) explains, meaning and context are inextricably bound up with each other. The code, the context, and the meaning can only be seen as different aspects of a single event. The level of context determines everything about the nature of the communication and is the foundation on which all subsequent behavior rests.

The meanings of the common words that make up our current vocabulary reflect the extremely low-context culture we live in and explain our behavior. We "share" on Facebook more personal information about ourselves than ever, but share less and less meaning. We are exposed to too much information with too little background to make any sense of it. We can "save" everything, but we remember very little. We take thousands of photographs, but have no time to ever go back to them. Our "stories" are animated three-second videos or graphically enhanced photos that disappear after 24 hours. The last thing our mobiles are is "phones," and nobody answers them anymore. We prefer to "text," but there is less and less text in our messages and more and more emoji, Bitmoji, reaction gifs, photos, videos, and links. We prefer asynchronous interactions that allow us to do other things simultaneously, to tend to additional contexts, offline and on—email, FaceTime, and more. When texting gets too laborious, we revert to talking. I have watched students conducting long WhatsApp "conversations," listening to recorded messages and recording their replies, and wondered—Why not just call?

I thoroughly appreciate the advantages of asynchronous communication. There are benefits to people not expecting an immediate response to others' messages, allowing them to reply when it suits them with better thought-out messages. However, I am not sure what is gained by the split second that separates the playing of the incoming message from the recording of the outgoing message. I suppose it has to do with millennials' phone phobia, as their fear of answering the phone and sometimes of its actual ringing can generate anxieties about having to speak, perform, and converse.

As a millennial herself explains (Demkes, 2021), if they answer the phone, they have to be grown-up and responsible for whatever the caller throws at them, and they fear not being good enough. It is like being on live television with no room for mistakes. They are not crazy about voice messages either. Their reactions to them can be postponed. But generally, the idea of not knowing what the voice message is about terrifies them. The looming criticism that induces their anxiety can be eased only by sending an accompanying text, preferably preceding the recorded one, clarifying what the voice message is about. When you are context-blind, the world is frightening.

What these young people need in order to cope with voice messages is what I.A. Richards called "feedforward." I.A. Richards introduced the term in 1951 at the 8th Macy Conference on Cybernetics and it was later used by McLuhan (Logan, 2015). One way of understanding the concept is that it involves providing the context before providing the message, so that the message will be understood. As opposed to feedback that is reactive, feedforward is proactive. It anticipates where one is headed and sets one's goals. It is a form of pragmatics—the use of context to assist meaning.

Remote teaching has provided me with multiple examples of my frightened, context-blind students. One student provided me feedforward and apologized for emailing me on a Saturday. Of course, he didn't need to apologize since email is used mostly asynchronously. Another student sent me a private WhatsApp at 2 am. Since I had created a group for our class to communicate more efficiently during the pandemic, she had my number. She didn't even identify herself, and I didn't know who she was, as she did not appear by name in my phone contacts. No apology this time.

Our culture is low-context and we are context-blind, so we can't see the gap that separates the calls for improving sex and gender identity equity and inclusion from the popularity of gender-reveal parties in America (Gieseler, 2018). We can't see the rift between the intimacy that characterized the traditional announcement and the pink smoke, tears, and jumping up and down of groups of adults that accompany "It's a girl!"

Context blindness clarifies the over-celebration of life events generally, and not just gender-reveal parties (Wong, 2018). When an important (if not the most important) part of an event is that it can be uploaded and shared on social media, weddings and receptions are not enough. These are now surrounded by engagement parties, bachelor weekends, bridal-party lunches, rehearsal dinners, pre-wedding bar nights, and after-wedding couple's showers. As if the stretching of traditional celebrations weren't enough, there are now celebrations of actions that were once not regarded as events at all. They used to be the actions that led to the events, like asking someone to the prom and now "promposals" or postpartum parties. When all of life is a sequence of pseudo-events (Boorstin, 1985) made to be shared on Twitter, Facebook, Instagram, and TikTok, pets' birthdays, divorces, and even job departures are occasions for a party.

Hall (1976) explains that contexting is the brain's ability to supply missing information and that it involves two processes: one inside the organism and the other outside. The first happens in the brain and is a function of either past experience (internalized contexting) or the structure of the nervous system (innate contexting), or both. The second (external contexting) involves the situation or setting in which an event occurs (situational or environmental contexting). When so many of our situations are mediated by technologies that are by definition high-context systems, and they keep getting better at contexting, our situational contexting is harmed, and we become increasingly low-context. As I shall explain in the following chapters, television has made us blind to one of the central elements of situations (space), and digital media has made us entirely context-blind.

References

Boorstin, D. J. (1985). *The image: A guide to pseudo-events in America.* New York: Atheneum.

Bullingham, L., & Vasconcelos, A. C. (2013). "The presentation of self in the online world": Goffman and the study of online identities. *Journal of information Science, 39*(1), 101–112.

Demkes, A. (Jan. 18, 2021). Why millennials have phone anxiety. *Medium.* https://medium.com/swlh/why-millennials-have-phone-anxiety-d83549eeec48

Gieseler, C. (2018). Gender-reveal parties: Performing community identity in pink and blue. *Journal of Gender Studies, 27*(6), 661–671.

Goffman, E. (1959). *The presentation of self in everyday life.* New York: Doubleday Anchor.

Hall, E. T. (1976). *Beyond culture.* Garden City, NY: Anchor Press/Doubleday.

Logan, R. K. (2015). Feedforward, I.A. Richards, Cybernetics and Marshall McLuhan. *Systema: Connecting Matter, Life, Culture and Technology, 3*(1), 177–185.

Nystrom, C. L. (2021). *The genes of culture: Towards a theory of symbols, meaning, and media* (S. Maushart & C. Wiebe, Eds., Vol. 1). New York: Peter Lang.

Postman, N. (1986). *Amusing ourselves to death: Public discourse in the age of show business.* New York: Penguin.

Ross, B. (May 3, 2016). Careful jaywalking saves lives. *GreaterGreaterWashington.* https://ggwash.org/view/41338/careful-jaywalking-saves-lives

Strate, L. (2006). *Echoes and reflections: On media ecology as a field of study*. Cresskill, NJ: Hampton Press.

Strate, L. (2017). *Media ecology: An approach to understanding the human condition*. New York: Peter Lang.

Strate, L. (September 1, 2020). Extravagant expectations. *Times of Israel*. https://blogs.timesofisrael.com/extravagant-expectations/

Vermeulen, P. (2011). Autism: From mind blindness to context blindness. *Autismdigest.com*.

Vision Zero Action Plan. (2014). City of New York Mayor, Bill de Blasio. https://on.nyc.gov/3ufH5Vc

Wong, A. (November 30, 2018). The over-celebration of life events. *The Atlantic*. https://www.theatlantic.com/family/archive/2018/11/gender-reveal-parties-life-events/577075/

CHAPTER FIVE

No Sense of Place: From Television to Social Media

I admit it made me mad to send my son to his room and find out a half-hour later, when I knocked on his door to say it was OK to come out, that he hadn't exactly been waiting for permission. He had forgotten I had sent him there and was happy watching a TV show on mute, listening to music with his earphones on, and chatting with friends on ICQ while I was still steaming about how he had dared to talk to me. Grounding a child or sending him to his room were regarded as effective disciplinary tools for a very long time, but their effectiveness has waned, since what made these forms of punishment work was that they cut kids off from all social interaction—a crucial part of their lives. Electronic media has enabled them to stay connected to the outside world from their rooms' confines and has thus reduced the importance of physical presence in their lives.

The telephone allowed us to communicate with others without being present in the same place. Television enabled us to be part of an audience at events without being physically present. Our laptops and mobile phones made it possible for us to study, work, and even date without leaving our rooms. We grounded ourselves. We sent ourselves to our rooms and loved it. Now we have to beg kids to come out of their rooms and look up from their phones.

As previously discussed, Strate connects McLuhan's concept of hot and cool media to Edward Hall's concept of high- and low-context cultures. In *No Sense of Place*, Meyrowitz (1986) connects Goffman's definition of situations to McLuhan's

(1964) idea that widespread changes in social behavior happen with changes in media of communication. He explores the common denominator that links the study of face-to-face interactions with the study of media: the structure of social situations. In other words, Meyrowitz takes a situational approach to the study of media to explain that electronic media altered the significance of space for social interaction. Physical spaces became less critical than before. Where one is, became less relevant to what one knows.

People behave differently in different social situations, depending on where they are and who they are with. Children stop giggling with their friends when a grown-up is nearby. And if a toddler falls on the playground, he will look around to see if anyone saw him fall before he starts crying.

It also used to be true that behavior in a given situation was affected by where one was not and who was not there. Since electronic media, however, we can be in places where we are not with people who are not there, and new social environments are created. In these environments, the link between physical place and social place is weakened. As we lose our old sense of place, we acquire new conceptions of what is regarded as appropriate social behavior.

Young people who grew up with television need less encouragement to "dance like nobody is watching." For us boomers, this was inspirational advice: to disregard the feelings that we experienced in co-presence situations in front of an audience, and to dance without being afraid of judgment or criticism, to act as if whoever was there was not there and enjoy it. Millennials, on the other hand, grew up in spaces that combined their rooms and the stages of *American Idol* and *Dancing with the Stars*, to say nothing of Gen Zers, who live on TikTok and dance for their millions of followers to watch.

Students in conversation used to change their language and adjust their tone and demeanor when a professor walked into a classroom. They don't anymore. They even continue their private phone conversations from the stall they entered at the school bathrooms, even after seeing me washing my hands when they walked in.

As Meyrowitz (1986) explains, many of the traditional differences between people (their socialization and authority) stemmed from their different sets of real-life situations and their respective distinctions between stage and backstage behaviors. Electronic media brought us all into the same place and blurred many previously different social roles. He summarizes: "Electronic media affect us, then, not primarily through their content, but by changing the situational geography of social life" (p. 6). The situations that he describes as a result of this new situational geography have increased and become the norm with digital media:

> ...students would see their teachers falling asleep in front of the television set, blue collar workers would see corporation presidents being yelled at by their own children, voters would see politicians have one drink too many, women would overhear men talking about strategies for interacting with women, and children would see the sometimes childish behaviors of their parents...We would be forced to say and do things in front of others that were once considered unseemly or rude. The behavior exhibited in this mixed setting would have many elements of behaviors from previously distinct encounters, but would involve a new synthesis, a new pattern—in effect, a new social order. An outside observer from the old social order might conclude that the people in this new social system had lost their sense of etiquette and even, perhaps, their morality and sanity. Yet that observer would, in fact, be witnessing the effects of a merger of social situations rather than a conscious decision to behave differently... More and more, media make us "direct" audiences to performances that happen in other places and give us access to audiences that are not physically present. (pp. 6–7)

Electronic media such as television brought about a new social order, but digital media seem to be eroding any kind of social order. The telephone and television weakened our sense of place, but we could still intuitively perceive situations, understand their definitions, and navigate them. We understood what someone meant by "you had to be there." We could imagine the intangible, the aspects of the situation that were hard to describe in words. With the contextual technologies of the digital age, we totally lost sight of situations, and the illusion that we are navigating through them is possible only because technology tells us to turn left in 200 meters and to continue straight at the roundabout, and it announces out loud that we have "arrived at our destination."

It sometimes feels impossible to navigate situations. How can one read the situation called "class" when a student walks in late and, holding balloons in her hand, encourages everyone to sing "Happy Birthday" along with her? This was once regarded as improper socialization of the student, but now situations are ambiguous. It is even hard to be mad at such students. They grew up in undefined, unlabeled situations, unlike the student from the 70s that Neil Postman missed in the 80s, who read a newspaper in class but covered it with the course textbook. This student obviously understood the definition of a class and knew that certain behaviors did not fit the situation, such as reading a newspaper. His covering it up was a sign of respect and good manners—alignment to or at least awareness of context. Class textbooks are now electronic, and they cannot serve as covers for media that belong in another context. Textbooks are "consumed" in class through the same laptop that not only also serves as notebook and pen to take notes, but also as the same window that connects students to their social rather than academic situations. They may be in a classroom physically, but their presence is elsewhere, on Instagram or at the "home" page of some Internet site.

Not only students are present in multiple places simultaneously; we all are, every time we look down at our phones in the physical company of others. Ong's (1967) concept of "presence," as well as Martin Buber's (1970) idea of I-Thou vs. I-It communication, are helpful in our attempts to understand ourselves as humans in the digital age.

Writing about presence before digital technology in the age of electronic media such as television and the telephone, Ong describes our sense of others' presence in the world as overpowering. He explains:

> For us the world is thoroughly "hominized"; human presence bears in on us from Europe and America to Russia and Japan and China, from Siberia through Cape Town and up from Tierra del Fuego to Hudson Bay. Indeed, our sense of almost total or closed human presence is so strong as to bring us readily to assume that it was always part of human experience. Of course, it was not. Modern man's sense of global presence, of a peopled world, is entirely novel, until recently an unheard-of thing, both a new burden and a new boon for our consciousness. (p. 296)

He adds that mediated human presence is so strong that we are the most interested in those who are farthest away, and that this is a kind of presence that does not require us to travel to meet each other and is realized within our media. When the media through which our presence is realized are digital media, however, presence requires a new definition. These days, we still don't have to travel to meet each other, but when we do travel, we are not entirely present where we are physically, as we are busy "sharing" what we are seeing and hearing with our friends and family back home in real-time, not just recounting on the phone from our hotel room at the end of an exciting day.

It is telling that there is no word for the sharing of live sound. We can "show" what we are seeing to our friends, but what do you call what we do when we allow them to hear the music we are hearing at a concert? If it's recorded, we can "play it" or "play it back," but this is true for both video and audio. "Streaming" or "livestreaming" have become the common verbs to describe the live sharing of both—fitting metaphors for the drowning feeling that ensues.

One of the things Ong (1967) emphasizes in the context of presence is sound. He talks about media's use of sound and explains that a live human voice on the phone or the radio creates a deep sense of presence and the present. That voice is "real," and it is on the air more than ever before (pp. 297–298). Along the same lines, Strate (2019) discusses acoustic space and explains that:

> ...because hearing is omnidirectional, acoustic space is all around us. Our position in acoustic space is at the center of it all, surrounded by what we hear. And this centering

> is ecological, as it places us inside the world, a part of our environment, integrated into our surroundings, requiring us to live in harmony with the world. (n.p)

Using Martin Buber's (1970) terminology, he says that we enter into I-You or I-Thou relationships with the world in acoustic space: relationships of reciprocity, of mutuality between subject and subject. As opposed to acoustic space, visual space locates us in a position that gives us the illusion of objectivity, leading us to objectify the world and treat everything in our environment as objects—in other words, in Buber's terms, to enter into an I-It relationship with the world. This is why, according to Strate (and McLuhan and Ong, whom he quotes), literate cultures saw themselves as separate from nature, which they tried to own and control. Electronic media restored to some extent the experience of acoustic space.

Digital media have changed this experience, as young people's preference of asynchronous communication and their phone anxiety reveal. We may be spontaneous and unrehearsed (or impulsive) on Twitter, but we like our voice recorded and edited. Like Strate, I find it odd and alarming that while opportunities to listen and choices as to what to listen to have increased, we have apparently gotten so used to smooth and edited voices on podcasts, for example, that public speaking has become scary, and the ability to engage in conversation and listen to others in face-to-face situations has suffered. Perhaps Gen Zers need encouragement to dance like nobody is watching, after all, as they are rarely watched live. Their TikTok performances are always asynchronous, edited, altered, and polished. They need to be in complete control of their I-It encounters. This is the opposite of presence since, as Ong explains, one test of presence is spontaneity or openness—"the openness of one consciousness to another in trust and love" (p. 298).

For a while, it seemed we could be witnessing the pendulum starting to swing with podcasts and social audio (Kafka, 2021). According to Lanier (2018), the degradation of context had not occurred in podcasts (at least as of the writing of his book in 2018), and it is fair to say that it hasn't to this day, but there seem to be some early cracks. Podcasters are still real people, known to the listener, and podcasts still build a sense of personality and context. They still rely on stores and subscriptions, so they maintain a person-to-person structure instead of a person-to-crowd/algorithm/hidden-manipulator structure. They are still managed by humans, driven by their desires and interests. Most of them have opening monologues that connect listeners to what came before and what will come after. They have "tables of contents" of sorts, and some (like Andrew Huberman's neuroscience podcast), inherently and through their organization bring back the idea of a prerequisite, or that in order to understand something on today's episode, you must first understand something discussed in a previous one. This means podcasts have context and contextualize knowledge for their listeners.

As for social audio, it looks like the spatial titles of these platforms such as Clubhouse and Twitter Spaces are a projection of our yearning for presence, for a "place" where we can experience unedited human speech, free conversation, and live dialogue. Maybe they are a reflection of the fact that we miss talking to each other, having the other person answer us in real time. We miss a sense of place that is more I-Thou and less I-It. So much so, that some are already predicting the fall of Clubhouse, explaining that its success was due to the pandemic and isolation, that the initial FOMO about getting an invite has abated, and that now that millions have been vaccinated, people don't want to sit and stare at their phones, but want to be outside, talking to real humans.

I don't know about that. I don't see people giving up the joy of staring at their phones. Either way, as Facebook tests Hotline (Perez, 2021)—a supposed mashup between Clubhouse or Twitter Spaces and Instagram Live, with video and recording capabilities—it looks to me like these originally-promising social audio platforms will probably become what Lanier (2018) feared they might. He wrote:

> To make the distinction clearer, I'll invent a way to ruin podcasting...Some crummy person could make an app that transcribes all the podcasts available in a store and synthesizes a new "artificially intelligent" podcast that combines snippets from lots of different podcasts that—as one example—contain the same set of keywords. You could say, "I want to hear opinions about x political candidate," or maybe about some celebrity...Then you'd hear a rapid-fire sequence of people saying things about the subject. You would not hear what had come just before each snippet or what comes next. The snippets would go by so fast, and there'd be so many of them, that even if a computer voice identified where each snippet was snipped from, you wouldn't be able to take it in...Podcasters would strive to come up with snippets catchy enough to be snagged and rolled into the sausage. There would be a lot of goofy cursing, ambushes, freaky screams and laughs, none of which meant much...Oh, and there would be ads mixed in...Armies of trolls and fake trolls would game the system and add enough cruel podcast snippets to the mix that your digest would become indigestible...Or, maybe your aggregated podcast will be a filter bubble. It will include only voices you agree with—except they won't really be voices, because the content will all be mushed together into a stream of fragments, a caricature of what listeners supposedly hold in common. You wouldn't even live in the same universe as someone listening to a different aggregation...If this scenario sounds preposterous and bizarre, look at what has happened to text, image, and video already. (pp. 70–71)

And so, podcasts and social audio of the days before Facebook seem more like exceptions to the rule of less sense of place—or worse, no sense of context.

It is hard to share Ong's (1967) optimism these days. Instead of minimizing in-group feelings that he contended electronic media would lead to as they connected the whole globe (pp. 301–302), social media have fostered extreme polarization and maximized in-group feelings. Ong also liked that radio and television, and primarily shows such as "Candid Camera," brought with them a whole new economy of spontaneity in production (p. 298), but cameras are not candid anymore. They are consistently and constantly in plain sight on every phone. We are not witnessing more spontaneous behavior but a complete disregard for the cameras, even when what they document is Derek Chauvin choking George Floyd to death.

Ong claims further that technological humans have been dehumanized only to a degree because gadgetry promotes humanization as much as it threatens it. In comparison to early humans who had to survive in hostile environments with no technology, humans in the electronic era live in a less alien world. Technology is part of them, allowing them to "move about and to take possession of all the world as of their home" (pp. 304–306). Ong should see us now, calling out "Alexa" for anything and everything, referring to it as "she," and conversing with bots as naturally as with humans. He referred to the social contacts of the electronic age as "decently personal and yet relatively noncommittal" (p. 303), but in the digital world of social media, our contacts are not at all personal, never genuinely intimate, and completely noncommittal. Some of our "friends" on Facebook are strangers we would not even recognize on the street. We post for them to "like" us in our I-It relationships with them, relationships of utilization or control between subject and object. It is no wonder that most social media platforms have abandoned the word "friends" and replaced it with "followers."

The thought that we may be yearning for actual human contact quickly dissipated for me the day we went back to teaching partially on campus after teaching remotely for a year. Students who had been vaccinated were encouraged to come back, and lectures continued to be Zoomed for those who were still home. After pointing out how exciting it was for her to be back in the physical classroom, one young woman proceeded to spend the remainder of our meeting looking at her phone, never once lifting her eyes to look at her peers or me. She had not just lost all sense of place; she was context-blind. The relationship between physical place and social situation had wholly vanished. "Place" is gone from our view altogether, and all that's left is a flow of information. All we need is power and Wi-Fi. Ong's statement is no longer true:

> The presence of other persons fills man's consciousness, as objects cannot. Situated among objects, a person may indeed find them interesting, but he responds only to

> other persons, other presences, who are not objects. In a whole universe filled with countless objects and occupied only by one other man alone, it would be to the man alone that I could present myself, establish a relationship of presence (p. 295).

Meyrowitz (1986) claimed that his theory suggests that a seemingly chaotic spectrum of social change happening at the time of his book's writing may have been an orderly adjustment in behavior patterns to match the new social situations created by electronic media (p. 9), but the social situations created by digital media make adjustment impossible and reality chaotic, at least partly due to context collapse on social media.

Context collapse refers to how people, information, and norms from one context leak into another (boyd, 2002, 2008; Marwick & boyd, 2011; Wesch, 2009). Meyrowitz (1986) pointed to this as an effect of broadcast media where journalists had to address large, varied, and invisible audiences. For example, Black Power advocate Stokely Carmichael used different rhetorical styles when presenting to black and white live audiences and had to choose one of these styles when speaking on television. This led to the engagement of his black audience and the alienation of white viewers.

Social media has taken the collapse of multiple audiences one step further to "the overlapping of role identities through the intermingling of distinct networks" (Davis & Jurgenson, 2014, p. 477). Collapsing contexts make difficult the smooth movement between networks and, in Mead's (1934) terms, across "generalized others." These all converge and require us to engage with family, friends, and colleagues simultaneously.

As Siva Vaidhyanathan (2018) puts it,

> Facebook scrambles our social worlds, our commercial worlds, and our political worlds. As we grow, we teach ourselves that we should not reveal some information about ourselves to our friends that we could comfortably share with our parents. We can trust our coaches and clergy with some things, but not our siblings. We forge social contexts. Sometimes these contexts intersect, as when a friendship blossoms in the workplace. But in general, we exercise autonomy over how we present ourselves among these spheres. Facebook puts everyone in one big room and calls them "Friends." (pp. 19–20)

In addition to the spatial dimension of context collapse, Brandtzaeg and Lüders (2018) suggested a collapse of temporal patterns in social media. They propose that our life-logs on social media are increasingly experienced as a collapsing of the past and the present, and that "time, in the context of social media, cannot be understood as a continued progression of events that occur in apparently irreversible sequences from the past through the present..." (p. 3).

Old user-generated content is known to resurface and sometimes backfire later in life, especially for social media natives who leave "digital traces" from their youth into adulthood. The digital traces from the past are unpredictably drawn into the present when, for example, a friend comes across an old photo and likes it or comments on it. The algorithms respond, and the photograph then appears in other friends' feeds as if it were something that just happened.

Self-documenting practices have existed for a very long time, of course. Journals, letters, and photographs capture fleeting moments and freeze bites of reality, thus also transcending time, but on social media, they collapse time, "muddling the distinction between the current version of a life narrative and previous versions." (Brandtzaeg & Lüders, 2018, p. 4).

As Rushkoff (2014) explains,

> Our analog technologies anchored us temporally in ways our digital ones don't. In a book or a scroll, the past is on our left, and the future is on our right. We know where we are in linear time by our position in the paper. While the book with its discrete pages is a bit more sequential than the scroll, both are entirely more oriented in time than the computer screen. Whichever program's window we may have open at the moment is the digital version of now, without context or placement in the timeline. The future on a blog is not to one side, but above—in the as-yet-unposted potential. The past isn't to the other side, but down, in and among older posts. Or over there, at the next hypertext link. What is next does not unfold over time, but is selected as part of a sequence. (n.p.)

The temporal dimension of context collapse, then, is not relevant only to social media. When everything is accessible to everyone, all the time, instantly, the original context disappears, and everything exists in the present tense. "Our electronic culture seems to be fixated on the present; the instantaneity of telecommunications communicates to us in the present tense…We thrive and live, up-to-the-minute, the on-demand, the just-in-time" (Strate, 2011, p. 92). We don't see where things came from or where they are going to, where they begin or end.

I remember the experience created years ago by a screen saver that randomly picked photographs on the computer from different times in my life. Family trips as a child and then as a parent. My birthdays and then my kids'. They all dissolved in and out of each other and floated around the screen in no specific order. They took me back 25 years, then jolted me forward 15. It was time collapse way before social media and #ThrowbackThursday.

Young people have been quitting Facebook for a few years now (Sweney, 2018). It is their parents' social media platform now, and it has become awkward. Context collapse is even more awkward online than in the real world, as on social media, we bring together "friends" in the thousands, and it's not over in a few hours like a wedding is. In the real physical world, at least in the past, parents, friends, exes, and colleagues each belonged in different situations and brought out different selves from us. Unless one abandons these virtual spaces, the self that results from context collapse is either a self-censored self that posts to the lowest common denominator and stays away from overly personal messages, or a self for whom there is no context, online or off—a context-blind self.

As Siva Vaidhyanathan (2018) explains further,

> This scrambling of our social lives causes anxiety and sometimes fractures relationships. Generally, it reminds us to be vigilant, imagining how the most hostile person might interpret what we are posting…Facebook is disorienting. We are a long time from figuring out how to live well with it. (p. 20)

Like Meyrowitz (1986), I believe that social change is always too complex to attribute to a single cause and too diverse to reduce to a single process (pp. 307–308). However, I believe that the thesis I offer in this book—that humans have become blind to context—connects many of the phenomena we have been experiencing. I think it is safe to say, 35 years and a technological revolution after his book, that we are unable to adjust our behavior because we have lost more than a sense of place; we have no sense of context. Our context blindness is not only a result of the context collapse in social media, but also of the delegation of our understanding and awareness of context to contextual technologies. These are at the center of the next chapter.

References

boyd, d. (2002). *Faceted ID/entity: Managing representation in a digital world* (Master's thesis). Cambridge, MA: Massachusetts Institute of Technology.

boyd, d. (2008). Why youth heart social network sites: The role of networked publics in teenage social life. In D. Buckingman (Ed.), *Youth, identity, and digital media* (pp. 119–142). Cambridge, MA: MIT Press.

Brandtzaeg, P. B., & Lüders, M. (2018). Time collapse in social media: Extending the context collapse. *Social Media+ Society*, *4*(1), 1–10.

Buber, M. (1970). *I and thou* (W. Kaufmann, Trans.). New York: Charles Scribner's Sons.

Davis, J. L., & Jurgenson, N. (2014). Context collapse: Theorizing context collusions and collisions. *Information, Communication & Society*, *17*(4), 476–485.

Kafka, P. (April 19, 2021). Facebook plans to go after Clubhouse—and podcasts—with a suite of new audio products. *Recode*, *Vox*. https://www.vox.com/recode/2021/4/18/22390742/facebook-podcasts-clubhouse-audio-launch-spotify-zuckerberg-apple

Lanier, J. (2018). *Ten arguments for deleting your social media accounts right now*. New York: Henry Holt.

Marwick, A. E., & boyd, d. (2011). I tweet honestly, I tweet passionately: Twitter users, context collapse, and the imagined audience. *New Media & Society, 13*, 114–133. doi:10.1177/1461444810365313.

McLuhan, M. (1964). *Understanding media: The extensions of man*. New York: Mentor.

Mead, G. H. (1934). *Mind, self and society*. Chicago, IL: University of Chicago Press.

Meyrowitz, J. (1986). *No sense of place: The impact of electronic media on social behavior*. New York: Oxford University Press.

Ong, W. J. (1967). *The presence of the word: Some prolegomena for cultural and religious history*. New Haven, CT: Yale University Press.

Perez, S. (April 7, 2021). Facebook tests Hotline, a Q&A product that's a mashup of Clubhouse and Instagram Live. *Techcrunch*. https://techcrunch.com/2021/04/07/facebook-tests-hotline-a-qa-product-thats-a-mashup-of-clubhouse-and-instagram-live/

Rushkoff, D. (2014). *Present shock: When everything happens now*. New York: Current/Penguin.

Strate, L. (2011). *On the binding biases of time and other essays on general semantics and media ecology*. Fort Worth, TX: Institute of General Semantics.

Strate, L. (2019). *"I hear you!": Comments on the sound practice of listening*. Global Listening Center. https://www.globallisteningcentre.org/i-hear-you/

Sweney, M. (February 12, 2018). Is Facebook for old people? Over-55s flock in as the young leave. *The Guardian*. https://www.theguardian.com/technology/2018/feb/12/is-facebook-for-old-people-over-55s-flock-in-as-the-young-leave

Vaidhyanathan, S. (2018). *Antisocial media: How Facebook disconnects us and undermines democracy*. Oxford, UK: Oxford University Press.

Wesch, M. (2009). YouTube and you: Experiences of self-awareness in the context-collapse of the recording webcam. *Explorations in Media Ecology*, *8*(2), 19–34. Retrieved from http://krex.kstate.edu/dspace/bitstream/handle/2097/6302/WeschEME2009.pdf?sequence=1

CHAPTER SIX

No Sense of Context: Mobile, Data, Sensors, and Location

Context collapse is only partly responsible for our context blindness. It is not only the collapse of space and time on social media—the mix of disparate social situations, friends from various social circles, and periods of life. Social media also contribute to our context blindness due to the volume of information and the extreme and disturbing content its algorithms encourage.

There is a growing call upon social media companies to take responsibility for offensive and violent content on their platforms. These companies are trying to develop policies and automated systems to manage extreme content and regulate what is allowed and what is deleted from their platforms, but they haven't been very successful at it.

Facebook, for example, processes 1.3 million posts per minute and, as described in a story on Vice (Vice News, 2019), it employs thousands of content moderators who have about 10 seconds to decide whether a post flagged by a user is offensive or violent. They can then ignore, escalate it (send it to a manager), or delete it.

According to the Vice story, moderators do not last on the job for very long, and some of them suffer from anxiety and PTSD. This is unsurprising, not only based on the volume of the posts they are required to handle, their content, and their tone, but also based on the posts' lack of context and the absence of context in the instructions for judging them. For example, Holocaust denial is covered by free speech in the U.S., but it is illegal in 14 countries, only four of which have actively taken up the matter with Facebook (Germany, France, Austria, and Israel). One cannot threaten heads of state, as they are regarded as a protected category, but it is okay to threaten anyone else. Animal abuse is allowed, as is child abuse, as long as the images are non-sexual, and the moderator does not deem them as having been shared "with sadism and celebration." An abused child is okay, but a sadistically abused child is not. Videos of violent deaths are allowed but are to be marked as disturbing, supposedly to protect minors. The live streaming of suicide attempts is allowed, too, as long as the video is deleted once the person has either died or been saved. The instructions for moderating sex seem equally arbitrary. Handmade art showing nudity and sex is allowed, but digitally made art is not, regardless of the actual pornographic content of either one.

What is the logic behind these instructions? In what context is non-sexual child abuse acceptable? On Facebook it apparently is, and when so much of our lives happen there, the conventions of the social network gradually spill over into the real world, and we become context-blind.

The solution to all of the ills that result from our use of social media, according to Jaron Lanier (2018), is to delete our social media accounts right now—which is, of course, unrealistic. There is indeed a preoccupation and discourse in certain circles around the need to disconnect from our digital devices and take a break from our data-saturated lifestyles. Some places, such as schools, are banning or at least limiting digital technologies in class. However, these calls to "disconnect" and "detox" are often adopted or appropriated by big tech companies themselves for their own profit and our eventual increased dependency on their products (Natale & Treré, 2020). For example, the Apple Watch, a device attached to the wrist and always carried around, was offered as an antidote to our dependency on other digital devices. One artifact is supposed to liberate us from the tyranny of another artifact, both manufactured by the same company.

Jaron Lanier's solution is not going to happen, just as Jerry Mander's (1978) call for the elimination of television did not happen. Postman (1985) believed Mander's idea was delusional and explained that people would not shut down any part of their technological apparatus, and that to suggest that they do so is to make no suggestion at all (p. 158). Instead, we need to be more keenly aware of the idea that a change in the form, volume, speed, and context of information means something, and to ask questions to ascertain that meaning.

Lanier is fully aware of this idea, and he offers a few arguments that may not lead most of his readers to take action and leave social media. However, they may raise their awareness of what social media have wrought, as they gather data about us, control our attention and our need for attention, intrude into our lives by making suggestions and imposing content, and manipulate our behavior. One of his arguments is at the heart of the thesis here: that social media makes what we say meaningless because it strips it of context.

Oobah Butler and his fake restaurant are good examples of what happens when context is stripped away on social media. In April 2017, Butler came up with the idea to try and get a restaurant that does not exist, verified on TripAdvisor. He made a website for his restaurant, The Shed at Dulwich, featuring photographs of dishes made with shaving foam and dishwasher tablets, and it was officially accepted and listed on TripAdvisor's site. Butler then spent six months asking friends to post reviews, and on November 1, 2017, the Shed was the highest-rated restaurant in London. He then wrote an article and made a documentary about the process, and the story went viral. Consequently, he was invited to appear on multiple TV shows around the world and decided that since he was being asked the same questions on every channel, and since people put up fake or touched-up versions of themselves on social media all the time, he could send different look-alikes of himself in his place to various interviews in Australia, India, and Bulgaria, and perhaps it would work in the real world as well. It did, of course. His doubles were not recognized, and Oobah got more invitations to follow-up interviews, more fans, and more new opportunities. He was even awarded a content-creation award, and he sent yet another look-alike to accept the award at the ceremony. We apparently all look the same in the context-less world of social media and increasingly aspire to achieve a generic similarity in real life, too. People undergoing plastic surgery to look like their Instagram filters or their selfies on Facetune attest to that. This is what has been called the cyborg look or Instagram face, and as Jia Tolentino (2019) of *The New Yorker* describes it:

> It's a young face, of course, with poreless skin and plump, high cheekbones. It has catlike eyes and long, cartoonish lashes; it has a small, neat nose and full, lush lips. It looks at you coyly but blankly, as if its owner has taken half a Klonopin and is considering asking you for a private-jet ride to Coachella. The face is distinctly white but ambiguously ethnic — it suggests a National Geographic composite illustrating what Americans will look like in 2050, if every American of the future were to be a direct descendant of Kim Kardashian West, Bella Hadid, Emily Ratajkowski and Kendall Jenner (who looks exactly like Emily Ratajkowski). (n.p.)

The author discusses the visual monotony or sameness not only of faces, but also of photographs on Instagram generally and InstaRepeat specifically. InstaRepeat is an account that posts grids of photographs previously posted by various users that are almost indistinguishable from each other. Their aesthetic—internalized by users—is based on whatever increases engagement and likes, and it exposes the damaging effects that the democratization of photography has had on originality.

The effects of the democratization of photography became apparent long before Instagram, with the availability of cameras for individual use that Daniel Boorstin (1985) discusses in the context of the difference between travel and tourism. Boorstin explains that tourism is the reproduced events of the same sites with the same people, only with different languages; he adds that the authentic traveler's experience has become impossible. Rather than being a journey in search of authenticity, tourism is a pseudo-event based on artificial images. Before leaving on a trip, tourists read guidebooks, go to the places recommended by them, and take photographs similar to those found in them.

Instagram has taken the sameness of places and poses one step further. In Los Angeles, people go on "Instagram Destination Tours" just to get a picture in front of a bubblegum-pink wall that has become one of the city's most famous Instagram destinations. The location bears no historical or cultural significance, but it attracts flocks of tourists who all take selfies in front of it, striking the same poses.

At a resort in the Maldives, we are encouraged to leave our selfie sticks behind, as the establishment offers "Instagram butlers" who help guests figure out how to get the best Instagram photos, pick a spot for them, frame their shots, and even take the photographs for them. They have an "Insta trail" that includes eight spots on two islands, and guests are shown the best angles to capture a specific moment and the best time of day for great lighting. There are signs throughout the resort that read "Instagram photo op this way." All the guests' photos end up looking the same, of course. Other hotels caught on, and at one in Bermuda, guests can look for selected photo locations and are urged to #PoseOnPink with the hotel's renowned millennial pink walls. All this sameness leads to an entropic visual reality with no differentiation of parts, a sort of visual equilibrium or homeostasis where there is no context to tell people and landscapes apart.

Of course, it is not just visual aspects online that lack context. Lanier (2018) explains that online, ordinary users (as opposed to advertisers) have no idea if what they say will appear or be streamed in sequence with racist, sexist, or otherwise prejudiced content. We don't know the context in which anything we say or write will be presented to or encountered by others. He explains further that the problem has become so pervasive that it is almost invisible—that we have given up our connection to context, and that what we say is contextualized and given meaning by the way algorithms mash it up with what other people say. The result of this surrender of context to the platform or the algorithm has led to extreme content, violent communication, and polarization of people and cultures.

> Your understanding of others has been disrupted because you don't know what they've experienced in their feeds, while the reverse is also true; the empathy others might

> offer you is challenged because you can't know the context in which you'll be understood...Your ability to know the world, to know truth, has been degraded, while the world's ability to know you has been corrupted. Politics has become unreal and terrifying, while economics has become unreal and unsustainable: two sides of the same coin. (Lanier, 2018, n.p.)

Social media are only one culprit of our context blindness. We reveal what we like, where we are, and what we are looking for through them. However, they are one of the various contextual technologies that are essential to what Scoble and Israel (2014) enthusiastically call the Age of Context. These include mobile, sensors, data, and location, and they are at the heart of this chapter.

Our blindness did not begin with these technologies. Traffic lights, for example, is a much older technology that controls human behavior as we delegate our decisions to them, and they regulate when we go and when we stop. We do not activate judgment, and we respond to the lights automatically. As it turns out, this leads to more, not fewer, accidents.

I live on a busy intersection in Tel Aviv and have witnessed probably dozens of accidents from my window throughout the years. I have not really counted, but from my general observations, I can say with a pretty high degree of confidence that the number of accidents or almost-accidents is the lowest when the traffic lights break down for a few hours. The honking will become impossible, and some of the curses among the impatient Israeli drivers may be heard all the way up to my third-floor window. But as furious as they may be, drivers are immediately more careful; they slow down more and pay closer attention as they try to make it through the busy crossing.

Without traffic lights or signs (and, apparently, without the swearing either), some places in the world have been experimenting with woonerfs—streets or squares where cars, pedestrians, and cyclists share the roads without the traditional safety infrastructure of lights, stop signs, curbs, painted lines, and pedestrian crossings to guide them (Jaffe, 2015). With all of these gone, everyone becomes more alert and focused. Vehicle speed automatically decreases, but there are fewer standstills. The number of deaths and serious injuries decline as traffic lights are replaced with common sense (BBC Staff, 2012).

Woonerfs are the exception. The leading trend is in the opposite direction: more automation rather than the use of common sense and situational sensitivity or context-reading on the part of humans. Tech giants such as Google, Uber, and Apple are using AI to create self-driving vehicles. These can understand their environments and navigate roads under different conditions, situations, or contexts, including the context of the emotions and cognitive states of the passengers and their interactions with each other. Hyundai Kia, for example, introduced in 2019 the Real-time Emotion Adaptive Driving (R.E.A.D.) technology. R.E.A.D. is an AI-powered interactive cabin that uses cameras and sensors to read passengers' facial expressions, heart rate, and electrodermal activity and then reacts and adjusts itself to their emotional state (Dickson, 2019).

We are losing our sense of direction and spatial context to navigation technology generally, and not only to self-driving cars. Spatial memory, spatial orientation, and mental mapping involve the hippocampus, and research shows that depending on GPS to navigate may negatively affect brain function, especially in the hippocampus (Gonzales-Franco et al., 2021).

Most of us rarely travel without GPS-embedded technologies anymore. These allow us to know our location all the time and help us avoid getting lost, but they also affect perception and judgment because they relieve us from figuring out where to go and which way to turn, from the need to create our own routes and remember them. We pay less attention and become blind to our surroundings or the context or situation we are in. Once available in hotel lobbies, paper maps are all but obsolete, and young people think they are as anachronistic as rotary phones.

Driving or walking around with Waze or Google maps impedes our engagement with our environment and adaptation to the present physical world around us. Aside from guiding us through a city, they also help us avoid traffic jams and find faster routes, but we notice how dependent we are when anxiety floods us if our battery dies or if we lose our data connection. We are left stranded. We don't remember any landmarks. We don't know how to ask for directions anymore. We are so context-blind that we literally only know how to follow directions blindly—to say nothing of quiet neighborhoods turning into traffic nightmares when Waze suggests an alternate route to all users stuck in traffic on a major highway who all find themselves similarly stuck again on the residential streets of a once-quiet town.

Self-driving cars and GPS are good examples of some of the forces that converge in contextual technology. Others to which we have delegated our ability to see and understand context include AI, sensors and wearables, the Internet of Things (IoT), and data.

David Brooks (2007) wrote as early as the year when the first iPhone was introduced by Steve Jobs—in a *New York Times* piece titled "The Outsourced Brain":

> I discovered the Sacred Order of the External Mind. I realized I could outsource those mental tasks I didn't want to perform. Life is a math problem, and I had a calculator…I had thought that the magic of the information age was that it allowed us to know more, but then I realized the magic of the information age is that it allows us to know less. It provides us with external cognitive servants — silicon memory

> systems, collaborative online filters, consumer preference algorithms, and networked knowledge. We can burden these servants and liberate ourselves…I have relinquished control over my decisions to the universal mind. I have fused with the knowledge of the cybersphere and entered the bliss of a higher metaphysic. (n.p.)

Control over our decisions has increasingly and even more substantially been relinquished to all of the technologies developed since the smartphone and built on it, as it is always with us and equipped with sensors. These technologies are based on what is known as contextual or context-aware computing, defined in large part by Anind Dey and Gregory Abowd (1999) over 20 years ago.

Contextual computing is one of the dominant paradigms in technology—the idea that computers can sense and react to the environment the way our brain interprets stimuli. Context-aware devices are given information about the conditions under which they can work and react appropriately based on rules. Contextual computing enables technologies to sense the objective and subjective aspects of a given situation—where we are, who we are with, and our past experiences. It knows everything about our social lives, our interests, and our behavior.

Contextual technologies are combinations of hardware, software, networks, and services. They fuse mobile, sensors and social data, and deep understanding of users to suggest tailored, relevant actions that they may want to take. Search engines try to understand the meaning of individual search terms as well as the context in which they were used or the aim of the user. For example, if someone searches for "Mexican," are they looking for a local taco stand, or for the Mexican embassy in a given city? Our phones use devices like gyroscopes to detect movement and location-based data to power Google Maps and Uber. They can tell us what our walking pace is or the quality of the air we are breathing. They can tell from both GPS and their accelerometers how much activity we are getting. Aided by data from wearable devices such as Fitbits, they can predict when we'll be hungry and how much we should eat to counterbalance our activity.

Contextual technology knows us better than we know ourselves. Google Now can predict what we want based on our past and on contextual data. Virtual assistants are always listening, and they use what they hear to provide contextual services. In addition to listening for instructions, they are getting better at listening to our homes, too. They can turn the lights on when we enter rooms and adjust the temperature depending on who is there.

These contextually sensitive services raise some important ethical questions about our privacy and about corporate interests. When asked, these questions sometimes even lead to results, like the pressure on Google to stop enabling cross-site tracking and targeting of individuals outside its own properties (Kaye,

2021). My concern here, however, is what has happened to our capabilities and who we have become as humans due to their takeover of our ability to read and understand situations. The answer is that when technology is contextual, users are context-blind.

Artificial Intelligence is everywhere—image and speech recognition, navigation apps, smartphones, personal assistants, ride-sharing apps, etc. The increase in storage space in the form of clouds, the improvements in calculation capabilities through chips, and the access to colossal datasets through e-commerce and social media have made possible the creation of statistical models that can evolve when fed new information. Affective AI has taken the process one step further and applied it to emotions. Algorithms can now tell our mood from the way we appear. They train a deep-learning algorithm on facial data and offer personally targeted advertising for services that make us feel better or cheer us up or keep us happy if we are already happy.

A new AI language model—the GPT3 (Generative Pre-trained Transformer 3)—uses deep learning to produce human-like text. It can compose business memos and even write stories and poetry. It can produce amazingly human-sounding sentences that are increasingly harder to discern from text produced by humans. It synthesizes text it finds on the Internet and creates a sort of scrapbook from millions of bits and pieces of text that it then sticks together on demand.

Jerome Pesenti, Head of AI at Facebook, tweeted some examples of what GPT-3 created when prompted to write tweets from one word—Jews, black, women, Holocaust. "Jews love money, at least most of the time," "Black is to white as down is to up," "The best female startup founders are named…Girl," and "A holocaust would make so much environmental sense if we could get people to agree it was moral."

Synthetic text presents a more significant challenge than those presented by the manipulation of images such as airbrushing, photoshopping, or filtering. Text is more ubiquitous, it is more difficult to detect, and we have no context to distinguish it from human text.

> It's possible that we'll soon have algorithms reading the web, forming "opinions," and then publishing their own responses. This boundless corpus of new content and comments, largely manufactured by machines, might then be processed by other machines, leading to a feedback loop that would significantly alter our information ecosystem…algorithmically generated content receives algorithmically generated responses, which feeds into algorithmically mediated curation systems that surface information based on engagement. (Diresta, 2020)

Some of this is happening already. Customer reviews are the one metric people have relied on for some time to determine the quality and authenticity of a product, but many of those reviews cannot be trusted. Thousands of fake and paid positive reviews from bots and click farms have flooded Amazon, Walmart, eBay, and others, and they are getting harder to spot.

We are losing our ability to read context, based not only on automatically generated texts. Our social life now includes interactions with bots and chatbots and virtual assistants: conversational AI technologies. These assistants recognize voice commands and translate their meanings across different languages. Siri, Alexa, and Google Assistant use a mechanism of imitating real-life human conversations built on machine learning (ML) and natural language processing (NLP). They are configured to be as human-like as possible. In the process, they gain insights from the wealth of data available to them, and we lose our sight, our insights, and abilities.

These assistants tell us the weather, play us songs, and anticipate what we will need later. We ask them to set a reminder, and they will nudge us later to complete the task. Google has taken this even further with a new tool called Assignable Reminders that enables us to send reminders to someone else in our Google family group. It is a tool that enhances passive-aggressive communication between house partners as they are reminded to pick up the dry cleaning when they happen to be in the vicinity of the dry cleaners. Google Assistant will then check the errand off the list. Again, beyond potential privacy pitfalls, the more central question here concerns the impact of these AI-supported interactions on our relationships (Goode, 2019); it seems like the impact is one that increases our context blindness, as reminders to others by virtual assistants is context-blind micromanagement of households and family. We are blind to the context of, say, what kind of a day our partner is having or what would be a good time, if at all, to ask them to do something and in what tone. When no effort and thought on our part are exerted to ask people to do things through the technology, the reminder mode spills over into our relationships in the real world, and we are bound to end up reminding (or rather commanding) and talking to each other impolitely. The thought at Google to add to the protocol around the reminders, the ability to thank someone, lets us delegate our manners too, and only deepens our blindness.

In addition to Affective AI, there is now also Embodied AI that aims to give tangible or visible form to virtual assistants and create robots that can move, see, speak, and interact. Rooted in psychology, cognitive sciences, and computer vision research, the idea is that just as it is crucial to the development of the elastic and creative intelligence of humans to start as a baby grounded in a physical, social, and linguistic world, it is likewise crucial to train embodied AI agents—virtual robots and egocentric assistants (with first-person views or sensors and perception that encode objects with respect to those agents)—to learn in the same way that humans learn (Bermudez, 2021).

A company called TwentyBN claims to be introducing the world's first context-aware digital companion, Millie, a life-sized embodied AI agent and helper that interacts with people by observing and understanding the context they are in and what they are doing. She is marketed as the ultimate assistant offering personal care across industries, from retail greeter and product promoter to personal coach for enhanced skills-based learning.

Millie's character can take on many forms depending on context, with customizable behavior and aesthetics. If one places her in front of merchandise, she will urge customers to touch it. In the future, she will be able to act as workspace assistant, dance instructor, or even a child's learning partner. Moreover, we are told that she will play an emotional role for the lonely and offer companionship. She is designed with empathy. We are told further that with the reduction of human contact, such as in supermarkets with cashier-less checkouts, Millie is a first step in the company's mission to design interfaces operating on the unconscious principles in human-to-human interaction…this approach is essential to preserving our humanity. "Without it, we run the risk of having our behavior fundamentally altered to suit the needs of technology." (Twenty Billion Neurons, 2018).

Get it? To preserve our humanity, the company has created an embodied AI contextual robot for us to interact with and fears that without their design, our behavior will be altered to suit the needs of technology. All this sounds like GPT-3 generated synthetic text to me.

Virtual assistants are not the only devices listening to us these days, so how do they know which one we are talking to? Which one should respond if they are all designed to answer to "Okay Google"? The answer is context, and sensors play an essential role in deciphering that context. Google wants users to treat voice assistance the way they would another human in conversation. When people talk to each other in groups, they do not address each other by name all the time. They use more subtle cues like eye contact or body language to figure out who is talking to whom. In conversation with listening devices, these cues are handled by sensors that help the devices understand whose turn it is to respond to our commands.

Sensors measure and report on change, and in so doing they mimic our human senses. They are being attached to all kinds of objects so they can share what they observe.

For example, Google already uses the sensors in our phones. If the phone is in our hand, we probably want it to respond. If it is resting on our desk, we are probably talking to our Google Home. If we ask Google's Assistant to send a text message, we are likely addressing our phone and not the smart speaker in our kitchen (Roettgers, 2017).

Sensors are used in multiple settings; they are used in stores in retail to know what customers are buying and anticipate what they will want on their next visit, and in traffic, they are embedded in Advanced Driver Assistance Systems. My car came equipped with such a system. Such systems are mandatory in every new car in Israel since 2018. It is loud, and I cannot lower its volume, which is part of the point, to be annoying, so I stop doing whatever made it beep or whistle loudly. I have been trained by the algorithm, but only to some extent. I have become better at slowing down earlier when getting closer to cars ahead. However, this contextual technology may understand cars, roads, and traffic, but it does not understand cultural context. The left or right signal is meant to let drivers know that one wants to cross over to their lane, but In Israel, it is actually a signal for the other driver to accelerate and not let one into their lane rather than to slow down to allow it. So, the road is one area where we are not wholly context-blind yet. Despite my Driver Assistance System, I insist on reading the situation on the road myself to cut off others successfully without blinking. I don't mind the deafening beeps anymore; I've stopped hearing them. I am startled, though when Mobileye beeps as it misidentifies electricity poles along the highway as humans trying to cross.

It will be interesting to see what happens to Israelis when self-driving cars take over and allow other drivers to cut the line and integrate into their lane. This will, of course, not be out of politeness, but out of algorithmic calculations. Still, I wonder if these cars may change cultural temperaments, and a weird calm may come to overtake Israeli roads and highways.

Sensors also provide context awareness for IoT, a concept developed about 20 years ago by Kevin Ashton, an MIT technology pioneer. The concept revolves around the idea of inanimate objects talking with humans and with each other over the Internet. IoT includes smart homes equipped with smart thermostats and doorbells, smart kitchen appliances, and smart bathroom fixtures. These "things" have Wi-Fi connectivity that makes it possible to lock doors remotely if we forgot to when we left for work or preheat our ovens on our way home from work.

I got an expensive present from my dentist (also my friend): a smart electric toothbrush. I do not know how smart it actually is because I haven't yet used it. I did read the information on the company's site that I reached by scanning the QR code on the box and found that the brush connects with an app that will track how long and how thoroughly I brush my teeth. It automatically buzzes or shuts off once I have hit the target time. The sensors in the handles detect the brush head's position, and they report to the app where in the mouth I have brushed and what I have neglected. The app displays this information in animations of my mouth on my mobile phone attached to my bathroom mirror to correct my course, and the pressure sensors alert me when I brush too hard so that I do not hurt my gums. Maybe I haven't used it because it is awkward and humiliating—a feeling that is, in and of itself, perhaps a good sign that I am not entirely context-blind yet. The first signs of my own blindness appeared a few years ago when, on a mission (again) to lose weight, I bought a Fitbit and recorded everything I ate, every step I took, and every run I went for. I lost some weight and got back in shape, but I stopped using it when I realized it had taken over my life. A ten-kilometer run that once would have felt like a real achievement did not count because it was not recorded, as I had forgotten my Fitbit at home.

IoT is everywhere. It is used for fitness and health, leisure, business efficiency, socializing and meeting new people, and more. It now exists also in the form of digital pills or ingestible sensors that transmit medical data from inside our bodies. The pills serve various purposes such as imaging, gas sensing, medication monitoring, and electrochemical sensing, and they can collect data from the oral cavity, esophagus, stomach, and colon.

There is now also Social Sensing in IoT. Social Sensing is the collection, processing, and analysis of data from social media and Internet communications that leads to insights into user interactions. Social Sensing uses knowledge from cyber-physical computing, sociology, sensor networks, social networks, cognition, data mining, estimation theory, data fusion, information theory, linguistics, machine learning, behavioral economics, and other fields. Social Sensing is used to understand issues ranging from radicalization by propaganda to potential election manipulation in democracies. It is helpful for real-time monitoring, prediction, and identification of events and for studying opinions, sentiments, moods, and emotions (Ducange & Fazzolari, 2017; Pandharipande, 2021; Wang et al., 2019).

These sensors and "things" create immense amounts of data, and data has limited to no value without context. Contextualization transforms senseless data into information, leading to insights that enable decision-making by technology. Applications gather and analyze data, detect human-based meaning from it, visualize it, and apply it to real situations in our daily lives—and as they get better at contextualizing, we get worse. Just about everything we use online comes to us from data. As Scoble and Israel (2014) call it, data is the oxygen of the Age of Context. It is everywhere and essential, but it has made us blind. When one searches for "context awareness" on Google, all the results concern technology's awareness of context, not humans'. As Jaron Lanier expressed it in an interview (Sterling, 2016):

> One thing that bugs me is the way context is lost. You start discovering new music or new culture in very particular ways. Algorithms become your guide. If an algorithm

> calculates that you may like a piece of music, it will recommend it to you. That makes the algorithm the master of context for humanity. It tends to remove culture from its context, and context is everything. The structure of the Net itself has become the context instead of real people or the real world. That's a really big deal. (n.p.)

How big a deal it has turned out to be that the structure of the Internet has become the context, rather than humans or the wider world, is at the heart of Part III, where the symptoms of context blindness are presented and discussed.

References

BBC Staff. (May 16, 2012). Viewpoint: Is it time to get rid of traffic lights? *BBC News Magazine.* https://www.bbc.com/news/magazine-18072259

Bermudez, L. (February 9, 2021). Overview of embodied artificial intelligence. *Medium.* https://medium.com/machinevision/overview-of-embodied-artificial-intelligence-b7f19d18022

Boorstin, D. J. (1985). *The image: A guide to pseudo-events in America.* New York: Atheneum.

Brooks, David. (October 26, 2007). The outsourced brain. *The New York Times.* https://www.nytimes.com/2007/10/26/opinion/26brooks.html

Dey, A. K., & Abowd, G. D. (1999). The context toolkit: Aiding the development of context-aware applications. Proceedings of the Conference on Human Factors in Computing Systems (CHI), New York: ACM Press (pp. 431–441).

Dickson, B. (November 28, 2019). Your next car will be watching you more than it's watching the road. *Gizmodo.* https://gizmodo.com/your-next-car-will-be-watching-you-more-than-its-watchi-1840055386

Diresta, R. (July 31, 2020). AI-generated text is the scariest deepfake of All. *Wired.* https://www.wired.com/story/ai-generated-text-is-the-scariest-deepfake-of-all/

Ducange, P., & Fazzolari, M. (2017, October). Social sensing and sentiment analysis: Using social media as useful information source. In Proceedings of *2017 International Conference on Smart Systems and Technologies (SST)* (pp. 301–306). https://doi.org/10.1109/sst.2017.8188714

Gonzales-Franco, M., Clemenson, G. D., & Miller, A. (May 7, 2021). How GPS weakens memory—and what we can do about it. *Scientific American.* https://www.scientificamerican.com/article/how-gps-weakens-memory-mdash-and-what-we-can-do-about-it/

Goode, L. (August 15, 2019). Google Assistant now lets you send reminders to other people. *Wired.* https://www.wired.com/story/google-assistant-assignable-reminders/

Jaffe, E. (March 23, 2015). 6 places where cars, bikes, and pedestrians all share the road as equals. *Bloomberg City Lab.* https://www.bloomberg.com/news/articles/2015-03-23/6-places-where-cars-bikes-and-pedestrians-all-share-the-road-as-equals

Kaye, K. (March 3, 2021). "We will not build alternate identifiers": In drastic shift, Google will end behavioral targeting, profile-building in its ad products. *Digiday*. https://digiday.com/media/we-will-not-build-alternate-identifiers-in-drastic-shift-google-will-end-behavioral-targeting-profile-building-in-its-ad-products/

Lanier, J. (2018). *Ten arguments for deleting your social media accounts right now*. New York: Henry Holt.

Mander, J. (1978). *Four arguments for the elimination of television*. New York: Quill.

Natale, S., & Treré, E. (2020). Vinyl won't save us: Reframing disconnection as engagement. *Media, Culture & Society*, *42*(4), 626–633.

Pandharipande, A. (2021). Social sensing in IoT applications: A review. *IEEE Sensors Journal* *21*(11), 12523–12530.

Postman, N. (1986). *Amusing ourselves to death: Public discourse in the age of show business*. New York: Penguin.

Roettgers, J. (May 18, 2017). Google's plan to make voice control work when all devices have microphones. *Variety*. https://variety.com/2017/digital/news/google-assistant-sensors-context-1202434876/

Scoble, R., & Israel, S. (2014). *Age of context: Mobile, sensors, data, and the future of privacy*. Patrick Brewster Press.

Sterling, B. (May 2, 2016). Meanwhile, in Jaron Lanier-land. *Wired*. https://www.wired.com/beyond-the-beyond/2016/05/meanwhile-jaron-lanier-land/

Tolentino, J. (December 12, 2019). The age of Instagram face. *The New Yorker*. https://www.newyorker.com/culture/decade-in-review/the-age-of-instagram-face

Twenty Billion Neurons. (December 3, 2018). Meet Millie, the first context-aware A.I. *Medium*. https://medium.com/twentybn/introducing-millie-the-first-context-aware-a-i-on-the-planet-d545eb6046b1

Vice News. (May 23, 2019). Leaked manuals show how Facebook decides if you see nudity or death. *Vice*. https://www.vice.com/en/article/d3xj4w/leaked-manuals-show-exactly-how-facebook-content-moderators-police-the-site

Wang, D., Szymanski, B. K., Abdelzaher, T., Ji, H., & Kaplan, L. (2019). The age of social sensing. *Computer*, *52*(1), 36–45.

PART III

THE SYMPTOMS OF CONTEXT BLINDNESS

CHAPTER SEVEN

Delusions: Flat-Earthers, Anti-vaxxers, and Global Warming Deniers

Part III of this book addresses the symptoms of context blindness brought about by contextual technologies. The symptoms include delusions, High-Conflict Personality (HCP), and hypersensitivity, fragility, and anxiety.

Some of these symptoms do in fact characterize people with autism. The proneness to delusions has displayed comorbidity with traits of autistic-spectrum disorders (Louzolo et al., 2017). Aggression rates may be higher in individuals with autism (Fitzpatrick et al., 2016), and upwards of 88 % of autistic children experience abnormalities due to sensory sensitivities (Black et al., 2017). However, the symptoms described in these chapters are used as metaphors to describe the context blindness that afflicts us as a culture—or, rather, as a species—in an age of contextual technologies. The symptom at the center of this chapter is delusions.

Conspiracy theories were generated, spread, and believed long before the Internet and social media. The anti-communist scares of the twentieth century, the Illuminati panics of the early nineteenth century, or the witch trials of the seventeenth century all flourished without the help of social media, as did conspiracies about UFOs and the assassination of JFK. Moreover, some scholars (Uscinski et al., 2018) claim that there is no evidence suggesting that more people believe in conspiracy theories because of the Internet. All researchers agree, however, that the Internet allows conspiracy theories to travel farther and faster than before, and that social media has brought about a true "infodemic" (Zarocostas, 2020)—a term coined to outline the hazards of misinformation during the management of disease outbreaks.

According to a study at the Annenberg Public Policy Center (Romer & Jamieson, 2021) that used a national U.S. probability sample in March 2020 and again in July 2020, 17 % of U.S. adults reported believing that "the pharmaceutical industry created the coronavirus to increase sales of its drugs and vaccines," up from 15 % in March; 32 % reported believing that some in the Centers for Disease Control and Prevention (CDC) were exaggerating the danger posed by the coronavirus to damage the Trump presidency, up from 24 % in March; and 38 % reported believing that the coronavirus was created by the Chinese government as a biological weapon, up from 28 % in March. Conspiracy theories are not limited to the source or actual existence of the COVID-19 pandemic, and they have increased since the development and availability of vaccines.

Like conspiracy theories generally, conspiracies around vaccines have existed since before the Internet and before the coronavirus, of course, but COVID-19 has provided a concentrated example of the role of social media in the dissemination and spread of anti-vaxxer theories. A report (CCDH, 2020a) from the Center for Countering Digital Hate and Anti-Vax Watch, found that up to 65 % of "anti-vaccine content" on Facebook and Twitter originated from twelve influencers within the anti-vaxxer movement. The report analyzed the content posted and shared on Facebook and Twitter between February 1 and March 16. On Facebook alone, the "Disinformation Dozen" content accounted for 73 % of all anti-vaxxer content posted or shared on the platform in those months. The most prominent anti-vaxxer influencer on social media, according to the report, is Joseph Mercola—an alternative medicine promoter who runs a multimillion-dollar online business selling dietary supplements. Another primary culprit is Robert F. Kennedy, Jr., the nephew of John F. Kennedy.

Another report (CCDH, 2020b) about the business of Anti-Vaxx called "Pandemic Profiteers" focuses on the financial gains of the dozen who generate profits by spreading misinformation. According to the report,

> …anti-vaxxers have received more than $1.5 million in federal loans through the Paycheck Protection Program (PPP) designed to help businesses through the Covid pandemic. Some leading anti-vaxxers are earning six-figure salaries for leading roles at anti-vaccine non-profits, including Robert F. Kennedy Jr., who earns $255,000 a year as Chairman of Children's Health Defense. The anti-vaxx industry's total social media following of 62 million could be worth up to $1.1 billion to social media platforms based on publicly available figures for the amount of revenue social media platforms make per impression or per user where that information is not available. (p. 5)

Another study (Germani & Biller-Andorno, 2021) analyzed the behavior of anti-vaccination supporters on Twitter and found that these supporters share conspiracy theories, use emotional language, and share their contents from a small fraction of profiles. According to this study, before his profile was suspended, Donald Trump was the main driver of vaccine misinformation on Twitter.

Trump's contribution to the context-blind war on science didn't start with misinformation about vaccines. In a 2017 story in the *Washington Post* (Sun & Eilperin, 2017), readers were told that the Trump administration had banned the use of certain words, including "transgender," "fetus," "evidence-based," and "science-based." The story turned out to be not entirely accurate, and in 2018 it was confirmed that the words weren't technically banned, but rather suggested as terms to avoid in order to improve funding chances (Cohen, 2018). Of course, there is a real difference between a ban on the use of certain words and a suggestion to avoid them. However, it is a distinction that doesn't make a difference if what we are interested in is what is hiding behind the ban or the recommendation.

One does not have to be great at identifying biases to unearth the assumptions of those recommending not using these words or their assumptions about the institutions that fund research. From the recommendation to avoid the word "fetus," we can guess easily enough what these people's position is on abortion. We can easily imagine what their definition of life is and when it begins, or how they feel about science if they would rather not see the words "science-based" or "evidence-based."

When the President of the United States is the source of misinformation, at least his "base" is more likely to believe what he means when he calls COVID-19 the "China virus," or to follow suit when he recommends drinking bleach as a remedy. When phenomena such as QAnon appear on platforms such as 4chan or 8chan, the blindness leads to insurrection.

In his book *Technopoly*, Neil Postman (1992) describes an experiment he used to do on his colleagues. After making sure that they had not read *The New York Times* that morning, he told them that there was a fascinating article in Section C about a study done at the University of Minnesota that found that a regular diet supplemented by chocolate eclairs three times a day leads to weight loss. The result of the experiment, he reports, is that about two-thirds of the victims believed or at least not wholly disbelieved what he told them. Postman explains that several conclusions might be drawn from these results, the first being that, as H. L. Mencken expressed it, there is no idea so stupid that you can't find a professor who will believe it. The second possible conclusion, as expressed by George Bernard Shaw, is that the average person in 1992 was about as credulous as the average person in the Middle Ages—that just as in the Middle Ages, people believed in the authority of their religion no matter what, and in the early 1990s, people believed in the authority of science no matter what. The third possible conclusion Postman arrived at is that the world was incomprehensible to people. This conclusion is, of course, ever truer 20 years later. It is more unlikely than ever before that we would be surprised by a fact (actual or imagined). More than ever before, we do not have a comprehensive and consistent picture of the world to make the fact unacceptable. The Internet, social media, and contextual technologies have "deprive[d] us of the social, political, historical, metaphysical, logical, or spiritual bases for knowing what is beyond belief" (p. 58). In other words, we have been deprived of context.

Some people even believe that the Earth is flat. They have their own social media accounts where they share this belief. In one especially viral post, they proudly announced that "The Flat Earth Society has members all around the globe." They are obviously deprived of the context that would allow them to notice the contradiction, so anything goes. We are context-blind, and full-blown delusions have replaced our credulity.

Only a context-blind person can claim that wind energy will not work because the wind doesn't blow all the time but only sometimes. This is what Trump told Sean Hannity, later adding that he "knows a lot about wind. If it doesn't blow, you can forget about television for that night." Only a context-blind public can elect a president who doesn't know that wind energy can be stored like other renewable power, and that it must replace fossil fuels before the Earth becomes fully uninhabitable, as David Wallace-Wells (2019) predicts, and sooner than we may think.

In a piece in *New York Magazine* two years before the publication of his book, Wallace-Wells (2017) explains that if readers' anxiety about global warming is dominated by fears of sea-level rise, they are barely scratching the surface of what terrors are possible, even within the lifetime of today's teenager. The swelling seas and the cities they will drown have dominated the picture of global warming and overwhelmed our capacity for climate panic, thus impeding our perception of other threats.

> Rising oceans are bad, in fact very bad, but fleeing the coastline will not be enough. Indeed, barring a significant adjustment to how billions of humans conduct their lives, parts of the Earth will likely become close to uninhabitable and other parts horrifically inhospitable as soon as the end of this century. (n.p.)

The other threats he discusses are heat death, the end of food supplies, plagues, unbreathable air, economic collapse, poisoned oceans, and the relationship between temperature and human violence and wars. He adds that no matter how well-informed we are, we are not alarmed enough. This, I believe, is because our context blindness has made us delusional. It is not, as he puts it, that we suffer from a failure of imagination; it is a failure of vision, a blindness in the face of all the scientific knowledge that is so readily available to us. He acknowledges that there is discomfort in considering a challenging problem that may be impossible to solve—that it is a problem of incomprehensible scale that amounts to the prospect of our own destruction. However, he adds that aversion arising from fear is a form of denial. Again, I believe this is not aversion, but inability.

Wallace-Wells himself asks why we can't see it but adds that this blindness will not last because the world we are about to inhabit will not permit it. He explains that climate scientists have faith that we will find a way to avert extreme warming because we must. They have confidence in the ingenuity of humans and believe that when we really see the world we have created, we will find a way to make it livable. For them, the alternative is unimaginable.

Wallace-Wells wonders whether this should be reassuring or if it is a form of delusion. I say delusion. Decisions are not up to scientists but politicians, and as we know, we should beware of politicians. On a record-breaking cold day, Trump tweeted that the country could use some of that good old global warming. He denied that global warming exists, claimed it was created by the Chinese to make U.S. manufacturing non-competitive, withdrew the United States from the Paris agreement, and mocked Greta Thunberg.

It is only fitting that a story in *New York Magazine* by the book's author ends with a note that reads:

> This article has been updated to provide context for the recent news reports about revisions to a satellite data set, to more accurately reflect the rate of warming during the Paleocene–Eocene Thermal Maximum, to clarify a reference to Peter Brannen's *The Ends of the World*, and to make clear that James Hansen still supports a carbon-tax based approach to emissions. (n.p.)

Only people who are not context-blind still insist on providing context. It is directed at others who, like them, are not yet blind. All the rest never get to the end of the story or the note.

There was human idiocy before the Internet, and there were conspiracy theories before social media, but the conspiratorial believers have an easier time spreading their conspiracies than ever before. They can claim that vaccines cause autism with greater ease than ever because distinctions between sources of information have been flattened online. This is context collapse yet again, which makes it hard to judge and marginalize fringe ideas effectively. Moreover, giant tech companies enable conspiracy peddlers because they boost traffic and profits.

In an essay for *Real Life* magazine on the "normalization of paranoia," Geoff Shullenberger (2017) writes that the medical definition of "delusion" is grounded in what a person's culture believes,

> so by the current definition if a delusion becomes the basis for a shared worldview, it ceases to be a delusion. It gains the approximate status of a belief that lies outside the mainstream consensus—like, say, the flat Earth —but is not viewed as symptomatic of a psychiatric illness. (n.p.)

I disagree. It may not be psychiatric, and it may not be an illness itself. But it is a symptom of the larger condition afflicting us: context blindness.

In a piece in *The New Yorker* titled "What if we stopped pretending?" Jonathan Franzen (2019) proposes that since it is already too late to reverse global warming, we should stop pretending that it isn't and do something else instead. He says that those younger than sixty have a good chance of witnessing radical changes of life on Earth like apocalyptic fires, epic flooding, hundreds of millions of refugees fleeing heat, and permanent drought, and those under thirty are guaranteed to witness it. So, he explains, there are two ways to think about it. One can keep on hoping that all of it is preventable and become frustrated or enraged by the world's inaction or accept that it is coming and rethink what it means to have hope—to fight smaller, more local battles that one has some realistic chance of winning. He says:

> Keep doing the right thing for the planet, yes, but also keep trying to save what you love *specifically*—a community, an institution, a wild place, a species that's in trouble—and take heart in your small successes. Any good thing you do now is arguably a hedge against the hotter future, but the really meaningful thing is that it's good today. As long as you have something to love, you have something to hope for. (n.p.)

This is inspiring, of course, but if we judge from the hate speech and polarization on social media, we are headed in an entirely different direction. These symptoms of context blindness are the topic of the next chapter.

References

Black, K. R., Stevenson, R. A., Segers, M., Ncube, B. L., Sun, S. Z., Philipp-Muller, A., Bebko, J. M., Barense, M. D., & Ferber, S. (2017). Linking anxiety and insistence on sameness in autistic children: The role of sensory hypersensitivity. *Journal of Autism and Developmental Disorders*, *47*(8), 2459–2470.

CCDH. (2020a). The disinformation dozen. *Center for Countering Digital Hate*. https://www.counterhate.com/disinformationdozen

CCDH. (2020b). Pandemic profiteers. *Center for Countering Digital Hate*. https://www.counterhate.com/pandemicprofiteers

Cohen, E. (January 31, 2018). The truth about those 7 words "banned" at the CDC. *CNN Health*.

Fitzpatrick, S. E., Srivorakiat, L., Wink, L. K., Pedapati, E. V., & Erickson, C. A. (2016). Aggression in autism spectrum disorder: Presentation and treatment options. *Neuropsychiatric Disease and Treatment, 12*, 1525–1538. https://doi.org/10.2147/NDT.S84585

Franzen, J. (September 8, 2019). What if we stopped pretending? *The New Yorker*. https://www.newyorker.com/culture/cultural-comment/what-if-we-stopped-pretending

Germani, F., & Biller-Andorno, N. (2021). The anti-vaccination infodemic on social media: A behavioral analysis. *PloS one, 16*(3), e0247642.

Louzolo, A., Gustavsson, P., Tigerström, L., Ingvar, M., Olsson, A., & Petrovic, P. (2017). Delusion-proneness displays comorbidity with traits of autistic-spectrum disorders and ADHD. *PloS one, 12*(5), e0177820.

Postman, N. (1992). *Technopoly: The surrender of culture to technology*. New York: Alfred Knopf.

Romer, D., & Jamieson, K. H. (2021). Patterns of media use, strength of belief in COVID-19 conspiracy theories, and the prevention of COVID-19 from March to July 2020 in the United States: Survey study. *Journal of Medical Internet Research, 23*(4), e25215.

Shullenberger, G. (May 23, 2017). Influencing machines. *Real Life Magazine*. https://reallifemag.com/influencing-machines/

Sun, L. H., Eilperin, J. (December 15, 2017). CDC gets list of forbidden words: Fetus, transgender, diversity. *The Washington Post*. https://www.washingtonpost.com/national/health-science/cdc-gets-list-of-forbidden-words-fetus-transgender-diversity/2017/12/15/f503837a-e1cf-11e7-89e8-edec16379010_story.html

Uscinski, J. E., DeWitt, D., & Atkinson, M. D. (2018). A web of conspiracy? Internet and conspiracy theory. In A. Dyrendal, D. G. Robertson, & E. Asprem (Eds.), *Handbook of conspiracy theory and contemporary religion* (pp. 106–130). Leiden, Netherlands: Brill.

Wallace-Wells, D. (July 9, 2017). When will climate change make the earth too hot for humans. *New York Magazine*. https://nymag.com/intelligencer/2017/07/climate-change-earth-too-hot-for-humans-annotated.html?gtm=top&gtm=bottom

Wallace-Wells, D. (2019). *The uninhabitable Earth: Life after warming*. New York: Tim Duggan Books.

Zarocostas, J. (2020). How to fight an infodemic. *The Lancet, 395*(10225), 676.

CHAPTER EIGHT

High-Conflict Personality (HCP): Tribalism, Identity Politics, and Cancel Culture

Aside from suffering from delusions, context-blind people are also characterized by High-Conflict Personalities (HCP). Every time we look at our phones, we are bound to encounter enraged posts, angry tweets, and infuriating news headlines. It feels like we are all constantly outraged. There is always someone on Facebook or Twitter waiting to pounce on anyone who disagrees with them about anything, and the social media platforms love it and use it. They are actually "hardwired" to make us act that way, without any regard for context.

Our smartphones are weapons for bullying and shaming—always in our hands, ready to be used to attack and polarize. Our identities and values are constantly in danger of being assaulted by social media mobs with their likes and retweets, aided by the algorithms that make them viral. Our anger reinforces the trench warfare dynamics that lead to the toxic call-out, cancel culture we live in (Wollebæk et al., 2019).

We had been intolerant of views opposed to ours before Donald Trump, COVID-19, and George Floyd's death, but all these underscored how technologies influence our behavior online and off. For example, Cinelli et al. (2021) explored the differences between various social media platforms and how each influences information spreading. Despite the differences in interaction paradigms among users and feed algorithms, all platforms were found to limit people's exposure to diverse perspectives and to favor the formation of groups of like-minded users, reinforcing shared narratives.

Since algorithms manage social interactions online, and since their goal is to maximize engagement, they maximize conflict as well, breeding disinformation and distrust (Caplan & Gillespie, 2020). Facebook's algorithms inherently segment users into belief communities that can be targeted with information that amplifies their political preferences. The algorithm rewards clickbait websites and tabloid-like sources of information, which often include highly partisan content, reinforcing insularity.

The balkanization of Internet communities and the rise in hyper-partisanship (Fletcher & Nielsen, 2017; Tucker et al., 2018; Marietta & Barker, 2019) has led to the replacement of the metaphor of the global village with the echo-chamber metaphor. The metaphor of multiple tribes has replaced the metaphor of the Internet as a global community, and collaboration has been replaced by hostility. When anger online is constant and all-encompassing, it manifests itself in the real world. The enmity has leaked from the online world into real life. Aside from the context collapse on social media, we now also experience the context collapse or collision between our online and offline identities. The antagonism is intensified as online and offline social networks, global and local communities, collapse into a common contextual ground.

This collapse aggravates our context blindness. We don't have the capacity to be in touch with as many people as technology allows. Our cognitive threshold and our ability to empathize are evolutionarily linked to a relatively small number of individuals (de Sola Pool & Kochen, 1978; Shirky, 2008). Additionally, as Bastos (2021) explains, social groups cannot grow as seamlessly as our communication infrastructure of omnipresent devices that allows connection to millions of people on cloud-based services.

> The disconnect between scalable technical infrastructure and the limits of our social networks, but also the social technology underpinning our social fabric, has produced asymmetric social divides including polarization and the breakdown of communities. In other words, as online communities scale both in size and geographic breadth, critical breakdowns in the limits of social integration, cohesion, and consensus reality may follow. (Bastos, 2021, p. 7)

As there is no consensus reality or shared context, we revert to tribes. Tribes are smaller groups that provide a more manageable context. In recent years, Turkey, Austria, the United States, India, and other democracies have elected authoritarian-leaning leaders who rely on tribalism for their power. Tribes fight other tribes. They watch over their interests and take care of their own. Perhaps Brexit marked the beginning of the collapse of the European Union, as some scholars believe (Scuira, 2017).

Israel has moved to tribalism too, as its former President Reuven Rivlin explained in a speech in 2015 that has come to be known as the Tribes Speech. He talked about the word "demographics" and added that those with a good ear would know that this use of the word is generally nothing but a presumably more polite way of describing populations other than one's own as a threat, as unwanted, or illegitimate. Sometimes the finger is pointed at Arabs, sometimes at ultra-Orthodox Jews, depending on the context. Then he moved on to provide some statistics.

First-grade classes in Israel's school systems were composed of about 38 % secular Jews, about 15 % national religious, about a quarter Arabs, and close to a quarter Orthodox. These numbers created a "new Israeli order," as he called it, a reality with no longer a clear majority or clear minority groups—a reality in which there are four populations, or four "tribes," essentially different from each other and growing closer in size, all of which raises questions about the future State of Israel. Will this be a secular, liberal state, Jewish and democratic? Will it be a state based on Jewish religious law? Will it be a state of all its citizens, of all its national, ethnic groups?

For now, each tribe has its own media channels and its own towns. Tel Aviv is the town of one tribe, Umm el Fahm the town of another, and Bnei Brak of yet another. Secular Jews, Arab citizens, and orthodox Jews respectively. It is not entirely clear what all these sectors have in common or whether they have a shared ethos or mutual values. The President then added that the language we use needs to change from "majority and minority" to "partnership," and that clarifying the essence of that partnership is the task of all of Israeli society.

Since the President's speech, these abstract principles have been articulated into concrete policy measures, but their implementation has not been easy. The parliamentary system of Israel means the President's role is primarily symbolic, and prime ministers make the decisions. Benjamin Netanyahu was the Prime Minister for 12 divisive years, and after Hamas and Israel began trading rocket fire and airstrikes in Gaza on May 10, 2021, riots broke out inside Israel, mainly in cities with mixed Jewish and Arab populations such as Jaffa and Acre, resulting in severe injuries and deaths, as well as widespread destruction of property.

There isn't much hope ahead, as the problem with tribalism is that it knows no real limiting principle. Anything that helps "us" and hurts "them" can be justified, no matter what it means for norms, balance, or the survival of the democratic system in the long run (Sullivan, 2018).

Tribalism manifests itself not only in party alliances but also in identity politics. Identity politics refers to people of a particular background—those with a shared racial, religious, ethnic, social, or cultural identity—forming political alliances that move away from traditional broad-coalition party politics and promote their own specific interests or concerns. It seeks to secure the political freedom of a particular ostracized population such as women, racial minorities, immigrants, LGBTQ people, and religious minorities.

The significant rise of identity politics is closely connected to the rise of populism around the world. When groups of people feel attacked, threatened, persecuted, or discriminated against, they retreat to an us-versus-them mode—a mode, as mentioned previously, which is aggravated by social media's business models and algorithms. It has even been termed "algorithmic identity politics."

As Apprich and his colleagues (2018) explain, "algorithmic identity politics" refers to how human prejudices re-emerge in algorithmic cultures (allegedly devised to be blind to them). By imposing identity on data to filter signals from noise, patterns become a highly political issue—thus, the computational term "pattern discrimination." The authors explain further that communality has been destroyed in a narcissistic culture of self-affirmation fostered by algorithmic personalization. Concealed behind the "echo chambers" and "filter bubbles" of social media is "a very reductive identity politics, which posits race and gender as 'immutable' categories and love as inherently 'love of the same'" (Apprich et al., 2018, p. xi).

Aside from social media, attention has also been paid lately to the role played by digital, contextual technologies in the mounting tensions between populations. Since AI learns by observing people, and society is biased and racist, almost all AI makes decisions that exhibit (and sometimes amplify) bias and racism. Our algorithms have the same race and gender prejudices as we do, and examples abound. A crime-predicting algorithm in Florida falsely labeled black people re-offenders at nearly twice the rate of white people. Google Translate converted the gender-neutral Turkish terms for certain professions into "he is a doctor" and "she is a nurse" in English (Ip, 2017). Microsoft's chatbot Zo was discontinued when it picked up some nasty habits. This over a year after Tay, an earlier bot, was taught to repeat conspiracy theories, racist views, and sexist remarks involving Hitler, Jews, Trump, and disrespectful portrayals of President Obama, among other things. Despite Microsoft programming Zo to ignore politics and religion, some people at BuzzFeed News managed to get the bot to react to the restricted topics, including referring to the Qur'an as "very violent" (Shah, 2017).

Algorithmic bias was also found in some self-driving cars that failed to detect dark-skinned pedestrians (Samuel, 2019). Google Maps is erasing Palestine (Chacar, 2018). Not only does the browser navigate to an unlabeled area, but its whole user experience disregards Israeli occupation. Even though it was recognized by a majority of United Nations General Assembly members in 2012, Palestine has not been labeled as such on Google Maps. While a "West Bank" label does exist, Israeli settlements there appear as if they are situated inside Israel. Palestinian villages unrecognized by Israel, are either misrepresented or omitted entirely. The map also ignores the segregated road system, including checkpoints and roadblocks, with its resulting movement restrictions on Palestinians.

This leaving out of populations is a form of symbolic annihilation by technology, but under the polarizing influence of social media, context-blind humans have adopted another form of "leaving out" or withdrawing support for individuals or groups under what has come to be known as "cancel culture." Cancel culture is the practice of banning or shunning a person (online or in-person) deemed to have acted or spoken in a problematic or offensive way. The debate around cancel culture is a heated one, to a great extent due to different definitions of different people or groups of what is regarded as objectionable or offensive.

Instead of banning them entirely, Disney+ added a warning on "The Muppet Show" episodes that contain "negative depictions and/or mistreatment of people or cultures," as the disclaimer reads. Disney added that "rather than remove the episodes, they want to acknowledge its harmful impact, learn from it, and spark conversation to create a more inclusive future together" (Spelling, 2021). In some of the episodes, it is clear why the disclaimer was necessary. For example, Joan Baez speaks with an Indian accent, and Johnny Cash performs in front of a Confederate flag. Other cases are not as clear. Blondie bandmate Chris Stein smokes a cigarette in the episode featuring Debbie Harry—not exactly a "negative depiction and/or mistreatment of people or cultures." In any case, parents can do as they see fit and heed or ignore the notifications, and if the warnings lead to conversations with their children about context, there is value in them.

The same is true of conversations between parents and children about Dr. Seuss books, some of which the writer's estate announced it would stop selling, as they portray people in hurtful and wrong ways. These conversations can cause people to re-evaluate the legacy of Dr. Seuss, parts of which should be honored and others not.

However, cancel culture has led to some unbelievable cancellations of cultural artifacts, all due to context blindness. A private Tel Aviv health clinic that decorated its walls with local artists' works was forced to take one down after complaints that the painting contained the Hebrew phrase "Death to the Jews." The artist Yaakov Mishori explained that the painting was based on the testimony of his mother, a German Jew, who on Kristallnacht (the November 1938 pogrom), saw the inscription "Death to the Jews" on the streets of the city where she grew up. This did not appease the critics, who saw it as "self-hatred and auto-anti-Semitism." The medical center removed the controversial painting following the complaints, and it even apologized if anyone's feelings were hurt (Shindman, 2020). Not Mishori's mother's feelings, of course.

Apparently rightly claiming that contextualization was needed before a retrospective could open, four museums postponed artist Philip Guston's retrospective until 2024 because of concerns about works that include Klan imagery—cartoonish hooded figures drawn in his later years. Instead of providing the necessary context for the relevant paintings in the exhibition, the museums' announcement stated that they were postponing it "until a time at which we think that the powerful message of social and racial justice that is at the center of Philip Guston's work can be more clearly interpreted" (Jacobs & Farago, 2020, n.p.). Could it be that we may regain our sight and stop being context-blind by 2024?

Cancel culture is also connected to the debate around the eradication of symbols and icons associated with oppressive systems around the world, inspired by the Black Lives Matter movement, which is the best illustration of the need to see and understand context. Beginning with Confederate statues in the Southern United States, a bout of iconoclasm spread to Europe too, and representations of slave owners, racists, and xenophobes were defaced or taken down.

Statues are among the most charged historical artifacts because they are a public, concrete expression of the politics of the time when they are produced. They are placed in public spaces, project power, and literally put leaders on a pedestal, positioning them as heroes. Thus, those in favor of removing statues see them not just as symbols of past oppression but also as representations of ongoing institutional racism. They believe that statues and memorials are affirmative representations that bestow legitimacy on the historical figures they portray and that they are offensive and constant reminders of injustice.

On the other side of the debate are critics who believe that we should resist the urge to wipe away the past; that tearing down statues does not undo history; that their removal allows us to disregard contentious chapters of history rather than engage with them and see them as learning opportunities. Some others believe that energy should go to demanding reparations and the allocation of educational resources to Black communities.

The concept of context runs through this debate. Contextualization is at the heart of calls to add inscriptions to statues outlining the history of the figure portrayed or moving them to museums where passersby are more likely to read the inscriptions. However, museums are not automatically willing to cold-store or exhibit these statues, and some believe that museums are not the appropriate place for massive reminders of the movements that made the erection of the statues and monuments possible; simply moving them to museums sidesteps the conversation that needs to take place. Also, they believe that putting monuments in context is not an easy task, that a simple label is not enough because museums convey authority. In a museum setting, statues remain powerful and imposing (Berger, 2021).

The High-Conflict Personality of contemporary humans manifests itself not only in our calls to cancel others, but also in our calls against cultural appropriation—which is, of course, also a result of context blindness and thus may be alleviated with the help of contextualization. As Malaka Gharib (2018) explains in her piece in NPR, sometimes it's OK to wear the clothing of another culture, while at some other times it's not. It depends on the context. When the author's husband came with her to a family party, they actually understood his wearing a barong (an embroidered long-sleeved formal shirt for men in the Philippines) as an act of cultural solidarity. Obviously, it is construed quite differently and regarded as appropriation if one wears the clothing of another culture to offend or make fun of the group intentionally or to assert power over them. To wear another culture's garb as part of a cultural exploration or education is different from wearing it just for fun on Halloween, without any background or context, or just because it looks nice. Intentions are important.

Now, contextualizing isn't always easy. I am not always aware of the history of every regional kind of embroidery in Mexico, where I grew up and where my parents are from. Is it cultural appropriation if I wear an embroidered blouse I bought when traveling around the country on my latest visit with my family? Is it acceptable for me to buy one for one of my friends in Israel and for her to wear it? How does one express that it is worn with respect? Or show that one is versed in the cultural and historical context of the given art?

Jenni Avins and Quartz (2015) explain that borrowing from other cultures isn't just inevitable but potentially positive in their piece titled "The Dos and Don'ts of Cultural Appropriation." This is an idea hard to grasp ever since, as she put it, "the term cultural appropriation jumped from academia into the realm of internet outrage and oversensitivity" (n.p.).

The authors acknowledge that there are reasons to be careful when dressing ourselves with the clothing, arts, artifacts, or ideas of other cultures. Still, they do not believe that appropriating elements from one another's cultures is in itself problematic. They think that is, in itself, naïve, counterproductive, and paternalistic.

> Such borrowing is how we got treasures such as New York pizza and Japanese denim—not to mention how the West got democratic discourse, mathematics, and the calendar. Yet as wave upon wave of shrill accusations of cultural appropriation make their way through the internet outrage cycle, the rhetoric ranges from earnest indignation to patronizing disrespect.

Avins and Quartz provide a few suggestions that are really all about context and common sense. Among them are, for example, that blackface is never OK because one should not dress up as an ethnic stereotype, or that it is essential to pay homage to artistry and ideas and acknowledge their origin. Also, one should not adopt sacred artifacts as accessories, and one should remember to engage with other cultures on more than an aesthetic level. Finally, it is a good idea to treat a cultural exchange like any other creative collaboration, giving credit and even considering royalties.

These are all sound recommendations, but the anger is not going away so quickly. Our context blindness keeps us furious, and we get really inventive, as the move from bullying to cyberbullying illustrates.

Bullying is probably as old as humanity, but the Internet has given it some new characteristics. Before the Internet, bullying ended when you left the environment you were in. Physical space and situation were significant. Nowadays, bullying follows you around wherever you go and at all times of the day. It is more difficult to contain and impossible to ignore.

If you're harassed on Facebook, context collapse means that all your social circles know about it; someone who persecutes you over e-mail or social media accounts is much tougher to avoid and dismiss. Cyberbullying is harder to escape, and since the Internet allows us to be non-confrontational and anonymous and there is no physical context, bullies do not witness the repercussions of their actions. This has made bullies out of people who would otherwise not be. As opposed to real life, on social media a bully does not have to be popular or physically dominant.

The Internet has created various forms of bullying such as flaming or using inflammatory language about someone hoping to elicit a reaction, as in "Sleepy Joe Biden" or "Phony Kamala," for example. Bullying can also take the form of outing or sharing personal or embarrassing information about someone, trolling, or posting derogatory or offensive comments about a person to get them all agitated, cyberstalking, and shaming.

We have become intolerant of anything that does not fit our own needs and wishes, and this makes for strange bedfellows. Yair Netanyahu, Bibi's son, became a hero at Breitbart after posting a meme rife with anti-Semitic themes about reptilians and Soros (who has spent a large part of his fortune funding pro-democracy and human rights groups). Soros is presented as controlling the world and being part of a conspiracy behind Netanyahu's family's legal problems. Ex-KKK leader David Duke came to young Netanyahu's defense, and the neo-Nazi Daily Stormer posted an article regarding the meme and called him "a total bro" (Haaretz Staff, 2017).

This kind of coalition between the son of the Prime Minister of the Jewish State and neo-Nazis is mindboggling, but the feeling is not sustained for long, and it goes away after a short while when news sites push the next astonishing headline on us. This is true not only of news and headlines, all of which are now "breaking news," but also of our exchanges. There is no lingering on anything. We don't ever argue until an agreement is achieved, or an argument is actually won. Instead, attention is diverted to something else to keep the conflict and the anger going. This is called "whataboutism" and, even though it is historically associated with Soviet propaganda (a rhetorical diversion by Soviet dictators to counter charges of oppression), it flourishes today, and there is no context to help us sustain an argument. We prefer shifting from a given topic to another, as irrelevant as that one may be to this one. Donald Trump used whataboutism as a tactic because, as John Oliver explains:

> It implies that all actions, regardless of context, share a moral equivalency...And since nobody is perfect, all criticism is hypocritical, and everyone should do whatever they want ... It doesn't solve a problem or win an argument. The point is to just muddy the waters, which just makes the other side mad. (Grant, 2019)

One such group of mad people are the Incels—involuntary celibates. They are a misogynistic online community united by their hate of women. They define themselves by their inability to obtain a sexual or romantic partner due to what they claim is systematic social hostility by women toward men. Their lousy reputation and primary media attention have been due to a particularly violent strain of misogyny that has linked them to several terrorist attacks. They are angry, sad, and frustrated, and their community operates in ways similar to anti-vaxxers and flat-earthers. They have their own sites, their own discussions, their own sources, their own reality and "post-truth identity online" (Baker & Chadwick, 2021).

It seems everybody is mad all the time. On the Internet, we can always find someone to keep us angry. We can become part of groups united by anger and quickly lose sight of the bigger picture, of context, of the outside world. The outside world is a scary place for context-blind people.

References

Apprich, C., Cramer, F., Hui Kyong Chun, W., & Steyerl, H. (2018). *Pattern discrimination*. Minneapolis: University of Minnesota Press.

Avins, J., & Quartz. (October 20, 2015). The dos and don'ts of cultural appropriation. *The Atlantic*. http://www.theatlantic.com/entertainment/archive/2015/10/the-dos-and-donts-of-cultural-appropriation/411292/

Baker, C. R., & Chadwick, A. (2021). Corrupted infrastructures of meaning: Post-truth identities online. In H. Tumber, S. Waisbord (Eds.), *The Routledge companion to media disinformation and populism* (pp. 312–322). London: Routledge.

Bastos, M. T. (2021). From global village to identity tribes: Context collapse and the darkest timeline. *Media and Communication, 9*(3), 50–58.

Berger, E. (2021). Contextualizing monuments and movies: Iconoclasm through the lenses of Media Ecology and General Semantics. *Anekaant: A Journal of Polysemic Thought, 12*, 2020–21 (Autumn) Special Issue – General Semantics and Media Ecology, pp. 35–38.

Caplan, R., & Gillespie, T. (2020). Tiered governance and demonetization: The shifting terms of labor and compensation in the platform economy. *Social Media+ Society*, *6*(2), 2056305120936636.

Chacar, H. (October 4, 2018). Lost in occupation: How Google Maps is erasing Palestine. *+972 Magazine*.

Cinelli, M., De Francisci Morales, G., Galeazzi, A., Quattrociocchi, W., & Starnini, M. (2021). The echo chamber effect on social media. *Proceedings of the National Academy of Sciences, 118*(9). https://doi. org/10.1073/pnas.2023301118

de Sola Pool, I., & Kochen, M. (1978). Contacts and influence. *Social networks*, *1*(1), 5–51.

Fletcher, R., & Nielsen, R. K. (2017). Are news audiences increasingly fragmented? A cross-national comparative analysis of cross-platform news audience fragmentation and duplication. *Journal of Communication*, *67*(4), 476–498.

Gharib, M. (October 26, 2018). When is it oK to wear the clothing of another culture? *NPR*. https://www.npr.org/sections/goatsandsoda/2018/10/26/658924715/when-is-it-ok-to-wear-the-clothing-of-another-culture

Grant, S. (November 13, 2019). Watch John Oliver break down Trump's three dangerous manipulation tactics. *Rolling Stone*. https://www.rollingstone.com/tv/tv-news/watch-john-oliver-break-down-trumps-three-dangerous-manipulation-tactics-116113/

Haaretz Staff. (September 9, 2017). Soros and reptilians controlling the world: Yair Netanyahu posts meme rife with anti-Semitic themes. *Haaretz*. https://www.haaretz.com/israel-news/yair-netanyahu-posts-meme-rife-with-anti-semitic-themes-1.5449468

Ip, C. (December 21, 2017). In 2017, society started taking AI bias seriously. *Engadget*. https://www.engadget.com/2017/12/21/algorithmic-bias-in-2018/

Jacobs, J., & Farago, J. (September 25, 2020). Delay of Philip Guston retrospective divides the art world. *New York Times*. https://www.nytimes.com/2020/09/25/arts/design/philip-guston-exhibition-delayed-criticism.html?action=click&module=RelatedLinks&pgtype=Article

Marietta, M., & Barker, D. C. (2019). *One nation, two realities: Dueling facts in American democracy*. New York: Oxford University Press.

Samuel, S. (March 6, 2019). A new study finds a potential risk with self-driving cars: Failure to detect dark-skinned pedestrians. *Vox*. https://www.vox.com/future-perfect/2019/3/5/18251924/self-driving-car-racial-bias-study-autonomous-vehicle-dark-skin

Scuira, L. (2017). Brexit beyond borders: Beginning of the EU collapse and return to nationalism. *Journal of International Affairs*, *70*(2), 109–123.

Shah, S. (July 4, 2017). Microsoft's "Zo" chatbot picked up some offensive habits. *Engadget*. https://www.engadget.com/2017/07/04/microsofts-zo-chatbot-picked-up-some-offensive-habits/

Shindman, P. (August 10, 2020). Tel Aviv hospital removes art with hidden message: "Death to the Jews." *World Israel News*. https://worldisraelnews.com/tel-aviv-medical-center-removes-death-to-the-jews-painting/

Shirky, C. (2008). *Here comes everybody: How change happens when people come together*. London, UK: Penguin.

Spelling, I. (February 24, 2021). Disney+ gave the muppets a warning for parents—but why? *Yahoo Lifestyle*. https://www.yahoo.com/lifestyle/disney-gave-muppets-warning-parents-160107278.html?guccounter=1

Sullivan, A. (February 2, 2018). When two tribes go to war. *New York Magazine*. https://nymag.com/intelligencer/2018/02/andrew-sullivan-when-two-tribes-go-to-war.html

Tucker, J. A., Guess, A., Barberá, P., Vaccari, C., Siegel, A., Sanovich, S., Stukal, D. & Nyhan, B. (March 19, 2018). *Social media, political polarization, and political disinformation: A review of the scientific literature*. William and Flora Hewlett Foundation. https://nymag.com/intelligencer/2018/02/andrew-sullivan-when-two-tribes-go-to-war.html

Wollebæk, D., Karlsen, R., Steen-Johnsen, K., & Enjolras, B. (2019). Anger, fear, and echo chambers: The emotional basis for online behavior. *Social Media+ Society*, *5*(2), 2056305119829859

CHAPTER NINE

Fragility and Hypersensitivity: Trigger Warnings, Safe Spaces, Trauma, and Anxiety

I didn't see my parents fight or even argue when I was a child. They made a conscious decision to present a united front when raising my four sisters and me. If they disagreed on something, they would not argue about it in our presence. I remember how frightened I was when they slipped, and I saw them argue for the first time. I thought they were about to divorce over something inconsequential and silly. I was probably 16 years old.

I had to learn by myself that harmony in a relationship is not the absence of conflict, but what comes after the negotiation, after the hard work involved in the resolution of disagreements. I had to learn to fight well.

Nobody fights well on social media, which has disrupted our arguing and battling abilities by obliterating context. On social media, we encounter fighting and screaming, threatening, name-calling, and storming out by millions of people who are all strangers. It is impossible to learn to fight well when the fighting happens among millions and there are no established conditions of attendance, no situation to provide context. Fighting and arguing and reconciliation require context—relationships, eye contact, listening, and reading situations. There is no such thing as "reading the room" to know how to behave when there is no room. In real life, there are consequences to walking away or storming out instead of asking if we understood someone correctly, admitting when we made a mistake, or apologizing. And forgiving. On social media, one can simply leave.

Public conversation has become exceptionally unpleasant. On social media, anything we say is bound to be greeted with nasty responses, and the constant nastiness has made people more fragile, especially young people. This emotional fragility is a result of growing up with social media, among other factors such as an overprotective upbringing. Instagram and Twitter are really good at spreading outrage because almost anything can be taken as an example of how dreadful the other side is if you strip it of context and hit "tweet" or "post."

This fragility began to manifest itself on university campuses where the call from students was that they needed protection from books, words, ideas, and speakers. Mechanisms were created for people to prosecute each other, boosting the culture of victimhood.

As Campbell and Manning (2018) explain, the moral conflicts at U.S. universities have bled into society at large. Young people are quick to police the words and deeds of others, who in turn claim that political correctness has run amok; both groups consider themselves victims of the other. They explain that these are not regular clashes between liberals and conservatives or the religious and secular, but rather a collision between a culture of victimhood and a culture of dignity.

According to Haidt and Lukianoff (2018), there has been a rise in anxiety and depression in students born after 1995, who are prone to see things as dangerous and threatening, including words and ideas. These are Gen Zers who were overprotected growing up and brought their call-out culture and norms of safetyism with them to college. There are now signs in every bathroom at multiple universities telling students how to report professors if they say anything students find offensive. Professors find themselves walking on eggshells around them and directing themselves to the most sensitive student in the room rather than the average student—even professors who have a proven record of creating a welcoming, inclusive atmosphere and cracking down on any displays of racism, homophobia, or sexism. With its disproportionate attention to single words, this new form of student activism is activism without context.

An attempt to provide context to what people say can be found in the Chicago Statement, a free-speech policy statement issued by the Committee on Freedom of Expression at the University of Chicago in 2015. Adopted by around 60 universities in the United States, the Statement aims to combat censorship on campus and protect free speech and the academic freedom of students and professors. The Statement acknowledges that the ideas of different university community members will often and quite naturally conflict, but it asserts that it is not the institution's role to attempt to shield individuals from ideas and opinions they find unwelcome or even deeply offensive. It emphasizes that universities value civility and promote a climate of mutual respect. Still, concerns about civility and mutual respect should never be used as a justification for closing off discussion of ideas, however offensive or disagreeable those ideas may be to some.

This is where the most profound rift between universities and students is found: between those who seek protection from negative emotions and those who see their job as fostering the ability to engage in debate and deliberation effectively and responsibly. The Chicago Statement may have helped some universities to function, but it has not changed the general atmosphere or the zeitgeist. In an era reigned by feelings, ideas or even words that hurt people's feelings are quite simply canceled, along with the person who uttered them.

The morality of soldiers in the army is an explosive topic in Israel, where military service is mandatory. Breaking the Silence is an organization of veteran soldiers who have served in the Israeli military since the Second Intifada in the year 2000 and have taken it upon themselves to expose the Israeli public to the realities of everyday life in the Occupied Territories. As they explain on their Internet site, they endeavor to stimulate public debate about the price paid for a reality in which young soldiers face a civilian Palestinian population on a daily basis and are engaged in controlling that population's everyday life. Their work aims to bring an end to the occupation.

A few years ago, my school attempted to hold an event and have a representative of Breaking the Silence come to talk with our students about their vision and answer as many tough questions as would obviously arise. The response was immediate, the resistance absolute, and no explanation about the importance of dialogue in an academic context helped. The faculty was accused of treason, no less, and the event was canceled. Inspiring material for an Israeli remake of Netflix's *The Chair*.

The ability to contextualize is essential to distance oneself from and debate the use of words and ideas. Context-blind individuals cannot see that the word is not the thing it stands for or represents. Thus, they cannot separate words from feelings, and their reactions are therefore signal reactions—automatic, reflexive, and emotional.

Talking about cancel culture and students' reactions to words, a friend who teaches at a university in Canada told me of her latest experience. She was teaching online and had asked each student to select a text or a poem relevant to the subject matter they were studying at the time. One student, a Black woman, read a poem by a Black woman poet but had to stop because another student interrupted the class to say that she had been triggered by the use of a slur used by the poet in the poem read by the student.

As I write these lines, I find myself looking up suggestions online on how to word the previous paragraph not to violate any rules or unintentionally insult any of my readers. I find people are grappling with these questions, all trying to be respectful but also all sounding very scared. One student asks in an academic forum: "I'm quoting a book and using a quote where the n-word is used. Later I'm going to have to read that out loud while my professor also has a copy. Should I censor the word when reading or writing it?"

I admit I find myself scared too. Is my use of the term "the n-word," three times removed in context from the racial slur, inappropriate on my part? It is not the word itself, and I am quoting a query online in order to tell a story about its use by a friend's student who was quoting someone else. Is it a sign of my racism? Am I being micro-aggressive?

Our need for protection from negative emotions has turned us into impulsive creatures. Like amoebas that detect and respond to stimuli such as light, so we react to words and ideas. We have become hypersensitive, and we believe we must strive to avoid bad experiences at all costs, to find safe spaces where we can feel protected, to come together to communicate regarding our experiences without feeling threatened or judged.

To feel protected is good, of course, but the problem is that we all feel we need protection from each other, and there is no safe space for all. We end up in safe spaces in the real world that are like the echo chambers of our social media accounts, surrounded by like-minded people, insulated from ideas that challenge our own (Furedi, 2018).

This is one of the objections to, or criticisms of, the idea of safe spaces. Others are that they are a danger to free speech, and that they are a danger to society too because we are raising a generation of infantile Americans. Brown University created a room with cookies, coloring books, bubbles, Play-Doh, calming music, pillows, blankets, and a video of frolicking puppies because a debate on sexual assault was taking place on campus. Another argument is that safe spaces blur the line between security against physical harm and being offensive. In *The New York Times*, Judith Shulevitz (2015) pointed out that once you designate some spaces as safe, you imply that the rest are unsafe.

Another criticism of safe spaces is that they threaten social movements because groupthink could get out of control and cause internal discord and crush unity. In this context, Conor Friedersdorf (2016) in *The Atlantic* warned that the rhetoric of safety could actually boomerang on activists if they insisted on living in a bubble.

Along the same lines, Furedi (2018) claimed that protest was once associated with enthusiasm for defying prevailing conventions; that it required a willingness to take risks and courage. This is the opposite of fragility and of hesitating to expose oneself to pressure. He added that those who combine the right to protest with the demand for a safe space are actually ridiculing protest. Once protest comes with a promise of safety, it becomes a performance, a theater of protest. The very principle of a safe space excludes the idea of real debate. A safe space quarantines people from unwanted criticism and judgment.

If people can't see the contradiction between protest and safe spaces, it is because their context blindness does not allow them to distinguish between news and reality, or between statements of fact and satire. Initiatives such as Facebook's to preface posts with labels reading "this is satire" hope to stop users from confusing satire with reality. The initiative is, of course, ridiculous, as the label itself kills satire.

> Take a look at the social shares for any news articles written by well-known satirical sites like *The Onion*, and you'll find plenty of people taking these stories at face value. In such a context, these posts are essentially a type of misinformation, even if their creators did not intend this. (Vincent, 2021, n.p.)

Some are rebelling, like Dave Chappelle in his *Sticks and Stones* Netflix special and Chris D'Elia in his tweet in 2018: "I'm not sorry for any of the jokes I've ever made in my life. I don't give a **** what you think about it. Figure your own **** out if your feelings are hurt." Perhaps when people are context-blind, there is no room for satire, or a sense of humor, or anything else that requires any amount of resilience, as the larger phenomenon of trigger warnings reveals.

Television and movies have had ratings for a very long time. These are mainly meant to alert parents that there are elements in the film or the show that might be considered unfit for certain ages. The warning was easier when the conditions of attendance to a movie were such that theaters could restrict entrance by not selling tickets to an R-rated film to young unaccompanied children under 17. Television stations could schedule content unfit for children later at night.

The conditions of attendance to the Internet and social media, especially since smartphones, have made it hard for parents to monitor and regulate the content to which their children are exposed. As for our own monitoring of content as adults, we cannot always predict what we will encounter. All we can do is metaphorically cover our eyes or look away the way we might when a scene in a movie is gruesome or scary and move on or scroll on.

A warning that some content ahead may be unfit for certain people can be regarded as polite, but trigger warnings are defined as statements at the beginning of a piece of writing that tell readers there may be potentially distressing material within it. The language used for these is very telling: we are all suffering from PTSD, so words or images are triggers, and the potential is for distress. Nothing less.

In a reality such as this, we have to be very careful. We may cause distress and trigger some bad reactions in our Facebook friends by posting something about the colorful cocktail we had after work. After all, in the collapsed context of our social media accounts, we can never know if someone is a recovering alcoholic. It has become potentially problematic to post "Happy Mothers' Day," since not everyone has living parents. Indeed, trigger warnings are already being made into algorithms, and online stores are asking customers if they would like to stop getting pushes about Mother's Day deals.

An online guide to trigger warnings (Atwal, 2020) begins by explaining why it is crucial to understand trigger warnings and assuring readers that using them for the first time can be daunting. "You can't help but worry about getting things wrong," it says to calm the readers down, but also adds that they should learn about them because

> at the most, it will help prevent someone from having a panic attack or worse…By putting choice back into the hands of those who have had traumatic experiences, they help create a safe space. This way, those with trauma can decide when and how to engage with the content. (n.p.)

Another guide to trigger warnings (Untonuggan, 2017) defines them as "a consent button for content" that puts choice back in the hands of what it calls survivors and lets them decide when and how to engage with traumatic content. The article provides a long list of warnings with their accepted abbreviations. For example:

> [T.W.: M.H., MI] mental health, mental illness; [T.W.: food] food (allergies, eating disorder, poverty, lack of food, etc.); [T.W.: E.D.] basic trigger warning for eating disorders, may be used in cases where food is mentioned a lot as well as disordered eating, internalized body shaming, etc. [T.W.: racism, systemic racism] systemic racism (see section on intergenerational trauma, above); [T.W.: ableism, systemic ableism]; [T.W.: violent imagery] violent imagery; [T.W.: flashing images] really good for people who get seizures and/or migraines, because ow. (n.p.)

There are many more, including anti-trans bigotry, gender essentialism, Islamophobia, antisemitism, Holocaust and Holocaust denial, white supremacy, gun violence, and war. We are taught further that sometimes people use abbreviations or a wildcard key so survivors can avoid certain words that in themselves can be triggering, such as N*zis, r*pe, su*c*de, or self h*rm. These are like beeps used to cover up profanity on television.

In what amounts to putting a PG13 on everything in life, the writer admits that sometimes she writes "[T.W.: I don't even know what to warn for, it's full of feels, but also very good content.]." As is perhaps to be expected, the article itself begins with a trigger warning: "T.W.// Talk and mention of trigger warnings." So, the mention of trigger warnings requires a trigger warning. It can get dizzying when the universe collapses into itself.

Trigger warnings are a sign of a deep yearning for context on the part of a context-blind population. A desperate need for feedforward (Logan, 2015). Before we went blind, when kids were frightened of a teacher, parents suggested that they imagine him or her peeing or brushing their teeth. Mine did, anyway. This allowed children to imagine intimidating teachers in a different context from the classroom or the test. It humanized them and reminded children that teachers were human, just like them. When a scene in a movie was creepy, adults reminded children that it wasn't blood but ketchup, or that the character couldn't die because that would be the end of the film. They activated the children's disbelief that had been suspended in order to enjoy the movie. We are now blind, however, and when everything is a trigger, it is no wonder everyone is shooting.

Twitter has blacklisted the popular account called "Journalists Posting Their L's." In Internet slang, to "post one's L" is to reveal a failure in public, deliberately or otherwise. All the blocked account did was collect social media posts and repost them without adding any commentary, tagging the journalists, or violating any of Twitter's policies against harassment. The mere positioning of the screenshot within the account provided context that was interpreted as hurtful, and the journalists' complaints led to the blacklisting.

The pressure of the traumatized public on social media generally led Twitter in 2020 to test a new feature of prompts that urge people to stop and reconsider a potentially harmful or offensive tweet or reply before sending (Butler & Parrella, 2021). Once prompted, users had a chance to edit, delete, or send the reply as is. In early tests, people were sometimes prompted needlessly because the algorithms struggled to understand the tone and sometimes didn't distinguish between potentially offensive language, sarcasm, and friendly teasing. The bugs were fixed by the contextually intelligent technology, making the users blinder but more polite and perhaps less anxious. The tests found that if prompted, 34 % of people revised their initial reply or decided not to send their reply at all. After being prompted once, people composed on average 11 % fewer offensive replies in the future. If prompted, people were less likely to receive offensive and harmful replies back.

As technology improves further by considering the nature of the relationship between the author and replier, including how often they interact, for example, it will continue to get better at understanding context, while the author and the replier get worse at it. "The Twitter prompts are an outsourcing of the superego, the little warning voice in our heads externalized as a piece of code" (Scott, 2021).

A few solutions have been suggested to alleviate the fragility. For example, as a replacement for safe spaces, brave spaces have been proposed (Arao & Clemens, 2013). These are places in which people can feel confident that they will not be exposed to discrimination, criticism, harassment, or any other emotional or physical harm. They are places where people come together to have tough conversations and hear each other out—even when that is challenging. In brave spaces, everybody is encouraged to speak honestly and critically from their own experience toward mutual learning.

This sounds like what universities are for, with a little bit of added courage. Before social media, no bravery was necessary, as the rules of each space were clear. The rules literally "came with the territory" and provided context to situations. As Nystrom (2021) explains, it used to be the case that if we knew where we were, we knew who we were in that specific situation, and how we were expected to behave in it.

Apparently knowing where we are is not enough to fulfill the expectations of others anymore. The rules of the Roland Garros tennis tournament, for example, include mandatory media interviews, yet these were what prompted Naomi Osaka to pull out of the French Open, quoting her social anxiety as the reason and explaining on Twitter that "anyone that knows me knows I'm introverted." She has since appeared on the cover of *Sports Illustrated*'s 2021 Swimsuit issue.

As mentioned in a previous chapter, this may be explained by the fact that Gen Zers rarely appear live on their social media platforms, and they prefer asynchronous communication that allows for a presentation of their edited, polished selves. Playing tennis is still a live performance. So is lighting the cauldron at the opening ceremony of the Tokyo Olympic Games. But they do not involve talking.

Various tools have been suggested and are being used in several settings to strengthen the fragile. These are discussed in Part IV.

References

Arao, B., & Clemens, K. (2013). From safe spaces to brave spaces: A new way to frame dialogue around diversity and social justice. In L. Landreman (Ed.), *The art of effective facilitation* (pp. 135–150). Sterling, VA: Stylus.

Atwal, S. (October 9, 2020). A guide to content and trigger warnings. *The Mix*. https://www.themix.org.uk/mental-health/looking-after-yourself/a-guide-to-content-and-trigger-warnings-37946.html

Butler, A., & Parrella, A. (May 5, 2021). Tweeting with consideration. *Blog Twitter*. https://blog.twitter.com/en_us/topics/product/2021/tweeting-with-consideration

Campbell, B., & Manning, J. (2018). *The rise of victimhood culture: Microaggressions, safe spaces, and the new culture wars*. Cham, Switzerland: Springer.

Friedersdorf, C. (April 22, 2016). The tools of campus activists at UC Davis are being turned against them. *The Atlantic*. https://www.theatlantic.com/politics/archive/2016/04/a-protest-against-the-protesters-at-uc-davis/479256/

Furedi, F. (2018). *How fear works: Culture of fear in the twenty-first century*. London: Bloomsbury.

Haidt, J., & Lukianoff, G. (2018). *The coddling of the American mind: How good intentions and bad ideas are setting up a generation for failure*. New York: Penguin.

Logan, R. K. (2015). Feedforward, I.A. Richards, Cybernetics and Marshall McLuhan. *Systema: Connecting Matter, Life, Culture and Technology, 3*(1), 177–185.

Nystrom, C. L. (2021). *The genes of culture: Towards a theory of symbols, meaning, and media* (S. Maushart & C. Wiebe, Eds., Vol. 1). New York: Peter Lang.

Scott, L. (July 14, 2021). Is social media making us better people? *Wired*. https://www.wired.com/story/is-social-media-making-us-better-people-tact/

Shulevitz, J. (March 22, 2015). Hiding from scary ideas. *New York Times*. https://www.nytimes.com/2015/03/22/opinion/sunday/judith-shulevitz-hiding-from-scary-ideas.html

Untonuggan (December 2, 2017). Trigger Warnings 101: A beginner's guide. *Medium*. https://medium.com/@UntoNuggan/trigger-warnings-101-a-beginners-guide-e9fc90c6ba0a

Vincent, J. (April 8, 2021). Facebook hopes tiny labels on posts will stop users confusing satire with reality. *The Verge*. https://www.theverge.com/2021/4/8/22373291/facebook-label-news-feed-page-posts-fan-satire-public-official

PART IV

TREATMENT

CHAPTER TEN

Therapy for Context-Blind Individuals: CBT, ACT, and Social Stories

It must have been around 1988 when Christine Nystrom, one of my legendary professors at NYU, spoke to us in class of the changes taking place in students over the years. The context was a lecture about George Herbert Mead, the I, and the Me. She was talking about the "internalized other" as the necessary precondition for self-consciousness and explaining that to be self-conscious and aware of oneself as an object implies that somehow one can step outside of oneself, observe oneself from a point of view other than one's own—that we are both actors and audiences of our own behavior. To be self-aware is to be capable of reflecting critically on actions that originate in different parts of ourselves.

The newer students, Chris bemoaned, were losing their self-awareness. She told us of a little experiment she did. She asked students to imagine and then draw a picture of themselves at the beach. She noticed that up until a few years earlier, students drew themselves as they would see themselves from the back, sitting on the sand and looking at the ocean, the sun, and the children playing with buckets and spades. Her newer students drew the beach, the children, the sea, and the sun, but did not draw themselves looking at all of it. It was as if they could not separate themselves from the things they were looking at. Perhaps it is not coincidental that ACT (Acceptance and Commitment Therapy) was developed in the mid-80s.

Acceptance and Commitment Therapy (ACT) is one of the models or intervention approaches of the third wave of Cognitive Behavioral Therapy (CBT). It is a psychological intervention that uses acceptance and mindfulness strategies and commitment and behavior change strategies to boost psychological flexibility. This flexibility requires approaching the present moment fully and consciously and changing behavior based on what the situation merits.

ACT includes the concept of the self-as-context—the idea that people are not the content of their thoughts or feelings, but rather the consciousness experiencing those thoughts and feelings. Self-as-context is distinguished from self-as-content: the social scripts or stories people believe about who they are and their place in the world. It distinguishes between myself as the experiencer of life, and the thoughts and stories that I tell myself about my life. Just as I am able to separate myself from the things I am looking at, ACT aims to help us separate our thoughts from ourselves (McHugh et al., 2019). The better we become at this separation, at metaphorically drawing ourselves on the beach thinking, and then our thoughts separately, the easier it becomes to see emotions within their situational context, to remain flexible and behave appropriately. This is what mindfulness aims to achieve as well. The mindful or self-aware person understands the difference between herself and her thoughts.

Based on Relational Frame Theory (RFT), ACT also illustrates the ways that language entraps people into pointless attempts to fight their own inner selves. Through metaphor, paradox, and various exercises, people learn how to connect with and recontextualize the thoughts, feelings, and memories they avoided previously, to accept them, and to perform the necessary change in behavior (Hayes, 2021). Some of the cognitive distortions rooted in language that RFT considers include either-or-thinking and over-generalization—the kinds of misuse of language that Korzybski (1958) points out and offers to counter with general semantics tools such as dating and indexing.

Although early research on ACT began in the 1980s, the therapy did not start to become widely disseminated until the publication of the official treatment manual in 1999 (Hayes et al., 1999). The increasing popularity of ACT since then can be explained by the publication of ACT self-help books and media coverage and promotion of the therapy and may also be explained by the increasing realization that what needs treatment is humans' misunderstanding of (or blindness to) context in the changing symbolic environment created by new technologies.

As Nystrom (2021) points out, Mead was living and writing before the full force of the electronic communications explosion was felt—when not even television was available, let alone the Internet and social media. His theory of symbolic interaction is grounded firmly in the assumption of real interactions where people encounter one another and their environment in situations of co-presence, in the flesh.

Cognitive Behavioral Therapy (CBT), which psychiatrist Aaron Beck developed in the 1960s, has been one of the most popular therapies over the past three decades. However, the emotional reasoning of Gen Zers, overly in touch with their feelings, has made them feel overwhelmed by their problems. According to a survey conducted in 2019 by the health service company Cigna (Hijiard, 2019), America is undergoing a "loneliness epidemic," with almost 50 % of participants feeling lonely. The survey included over 20,000 adults and found that 43 % of the participants sometimes or always feel isolated from others and that their relationships are not meaningful. Also, 27 % rarely or never feel as though people really understand and connect with them. Only 53 % of participants felt that they have meaningful in-person social interactions on a daily basis. The study found that loneliness scores rose among the younger generations, with the youngest (Gen Z) feeling the loneliest. The researchers attribute these numbers to several factors, one of which is people's increasing reliance on social media for their interactions rather than face-to-face contact.

Haidt and Lukianoff (2018) explained that in addition to other factors, social media contribute to the fragility and the problems plaguing Gen Z. They recommend CBT as helpful in countering this context-blind generation's belief that one should always trust one's feelings. CBT generally has proven effective in helping people question their feelings and look for evidence. But ACT and other third-wave behavioral and cognitive methods emerged based on contextual concepts revolving around a person's relationship to thought and emotion rather than their content (Hayes & Hofmann, 2017).

Multiple tools are used with people with autism to help them with their context blindness. Some of them are developmental such as Play Therapy Training, the SCERTS Model (Social Communication, Emotional Regulation, and Transactional Supports Model), and the Hanen Program for Natural Language Development Strategies. Other techniques emphasize early intervention, including treatments such as JASPER (Joint Attention, Symbolic Play, Engagement, and Regulation). Others are behavioral such as ABA—Applied Behavior Analysis, while still others are educational such as Feuerstein's Mediated Learning Experience (MLE). Others are clinical therapies such as Occupational Therapy for Sensory Integration, Speech and Language Therapy, Physical Therapy, and Social Thinking.

Social thinking and social skills training tools include "Social Stories." These help people with autism understand different situations or contexts—including, lately, why, and how to wear a mask.

Wearing face masks has become a new norm in the COVID-19 era. Even though it was uncomfortable at first, we all got used to it and learned to deal with the discomfort, but what is uncomfortable for most can be intolerable for individuals with autism. Sensory issues and anxiety make such discomfort much harder for them to bear, so some places are using Social Stories to help them cope.

Social Stories were created by Carol Gray and later published officially by Gray and Garand (1993) to help individuals with autism understand social situations, expectations, social cues, new activities, and social rules. As the name suggests, Social Stories are brief narratives that give precise information about a social situation. These stories are tailored to elucidate social expectations using visuals and specific sentence structures. Knowing what to expect by using a Social Story can help individuals with autism successfully endure new situations such as wearing a face mask.

When creating a Social Story, three kinds of sentences are used: descriptive, perspective, and directive sentences. Descriptive sentences define the expected events where a situation occurs, who is participating, what they are doing, and why. Perspective sentences describe the person's internal condition or persons involved, and directive sentences are personalized statements of desired responses expressed positively. A Social Story about wearing a mask in public may read like this:

> When I go to the store, I see people shopping with masks on (descriptive). They are wearing masks to help stop the spread of COVID-19 (descriptive). COVID-19 is an illness that can make people very sick (descriptive). Wearing a mask can help protect people from getting COVID-19 (descriptive). I do not like seeing people wearing masks (perspective). It makes me feel scared (perspective). I do not like the feeling of a mask on my face. (perspective). It is uncomfortable (perspective). I will practice wearing my mask for a few minutes each day (directive). The more I practice wearing a mask, the easier it will be to wear (directive). I can practice taking deep breaths before I put my face mask on, and this will help me feel relaxed (directive). (AAoM, 2020)

As they are rooted in the idea of context, the instructions for creating a Social Story guide us to avoid using too many directive sentences, as they are ineffective without adequate contextualization. One is advised also to write in the first-person and at the individual's developmental level. Stories should include pictures or other visuals to supplement the text that fit this developmental level.

In the end, a story is a Social Story if it accurately describes a context, skill, achievement, or concept according to the ten defining criteria of Social Stories. It also needs to include planning for comprehension, planning a Story review, organizing the Stories, and Story re-runs and sequels to connect past, present, and future (Gray, 2018).

In her recounting of how she created Social Stories, Carol Gray relates a conversation she had with a boy named Eric. Carol had tried for years to teach Eric to raise his hand, wait for his turn to talk, and listen when others are talking.

Eric really wanted to stop interrupting and promised he would do so. However, for over a decade, he had never held his comments back or raised his hand in class before speaking. The same happened at an all-school assembly at which Eric interrupted the speaker.

When Carol reviewed the videotape of the assembly with Eric in what is called a Social Reading, they compared their perceptions of what had happened. Eric said there were two people in the assembly: he and the speaker. He did not mention the 500 students around him in the audience. Suddenly Eric's interrupting made sense to Carol. He was doing what she had taught him to do—to answer if someone talks to you. From Eric's perspective, he was attentive, responding to his teacher, who at the time was the invited speaker.

Carol's realization of what she had missed became a turning point, and from then on, Eric began to create a list of things he needed to do to stop interrupting: raise his hand, listen when others talk, and give others a turn. For the first time in any class, he raised his hand. He also was able to generalize the behavior to other settings (Gray, 2021).

As is evident at this point in the book, humans generally—not only people with autism—have trouble understanding situations, dealing with anxiety, and trying to read and understand context in an environment mediated by social media and replete with contextual technologies. For them, for all of us, to cope with the symptoms of context blindness and perhaps even regain some of our sight, what we need is not an understanding of the self-as-context but of media as context, to become proficient in context analysis.

Context analysis is at the heart of the discipline called Media Ecology, and its potential benefits are presented in the next chapter.

References

AAoM Staff, (Jun 9, 2020). Social stories as a means to teach mask wearing. *Autism Alliance of Michigan*. https://autismallianceofmichigan.org/social-stories-as-a-means-to-teach-mask-wearing/

Gray, C. A., & Garand, J. D. (1993). Social stories: Improving responses of students with autism with accurate social information. *Focus on Autistic Behavior*, *8*(1), 1–10.

Gray, C. (December 2018). The social story philosophy. *Carol Gray Social Stories*. https://carolgraysocialstories.com/wp-content/uploads/2018/12/Social-Stories-10.2-Criteria.pdf

Gray, C. (2021). The discovery of social stories (1990–1992). *Carol Gray Social Stories*. https://carolgraysocialstories.com/social-stories/the-discovery-of-social-stories/

Haidt, J., & Lukianoff, G. (2018). *The coddling of the American mind: How good intentions and bad ideas are setting up a generation for failure*. New York: Penguin.

Hayes, S. (2021). What is RFT? *Contextual Science*. https://contextualscience.org/what_is_rft

Hayes, S. C., & Hofmann, S. G. (2017). The third wave of cognitive behavioral therapy and the rise of process-based care. *World Psychiatry*, *16*(3), 245.

Hayes, S., Strosahl, & Wilson. (1999). *Acceptance and commitment therapy: An experiential approach to behavior change*. New York: Guilford Press.

Hijiard, J. (August 14, 2019). Study reveals Gen Z As the loneliest generation in America. *Addiction Center*. https://www.addictioncenter.com/news/2019/08/gen-z-loneliest-generation/

Korzybski, A. (1958). *Science and sanity: An introduction to non-Aristotelian systems and general semantics*. Lakeville, CT: Institute of GS.

McHugh, L., Stewart, I., & Almada, P. (2019). *A contextual behavioral guide to the self: Theory and practice*. Oakland: New Harbinger Publications.

Nystrom, C. L. (2021). *The genes of culture: Towards a theory of symbols, meaning, and media* (S. Maushart & C. Wiebe, Eds., Vol. 1). New York: Peter Lang.

CHAPTER ELEVEN

Therapy for a Context-Blind Humanity: Media Ecology as Context Analysis

I was born in the United States to Mexican parents. I grew up in Mexico from the age of three and moved to Israel when I was 15 years old. After three years of high school, two years of mandatory army service, and another three as an undergraduate at Tel Aviv University, I left Israel again to pursue my M.A. and then my doctorate at NYU. I studied and taught as a teaching fellow in the Department of Culture and Communication. The name of my program was Media Ecology.

I am the product of at least three cultures and languages. My mother tongue is Spanish. I was immersed in Hebrew in high school as an immigrant to Israel. I encountered the English of *The Flintstones, Romper Room*, and *Captain Kangaroo* on TV at age two, and the English of graduate school in my 20s. I can also be regarded as the product of an additional culture because my grandparents came to Mexico from Eastern Europe in the 1920s. I grew up hearing them speak and sometimes even talked to them in Yiddish.

I understand almost intuitively that language is a situated activity that does not exist in a vacuum. It is part of what Malinowski (1923) means by situational context—"the dependence of the meaning of each word upon practical experience, and of the structure of each utterance upon the momentary situation in which it is spoken" (p. 312). Or, in Wittgenstein's (1958) terms, language is a form of life that is constantly defined by its origin, purpose, and influence on the environment in which it occurs.

I suppose that my keen interest in context is a result of this life in three languages, a dozen different apartments (literally), in three countries on two continents. All of these have made it crucial for me to develop a more advanced ability to read situations than that required of all of us—to behave appropriately at a dinner party, a lecture, or a business meeting. Every person who has relocated for work knows this.

I have been aware of how aware I am of context from quite an early age. I remember thinking how different teenagers were in Mexico from my new classmates in Israel. The Israelis felt closer to nature, somehow. They walked home from school through empty lots where wildflowers grew, and they knew their names. I learned that it was officially spring, and Passover was nearing because the air smelled like citrus orchards. Mexico City smelled like smog, even in the 70s. Tel Aviv now smells like smog as well.

About a month after Passover, my friends would start to go to the beach straight after school. Beachgoing was recontextualized for me and became a casual activity, something you can do easily if you just remember to add a bathing suit and a towel to your schoolbag in the morning. During my childhood in Mexico City, it took six hours to get to the nearest beach, so it came to be connected in my mind with holidays and family vacations. Smell was significant here, too. It was part of what defined the situation. The scent of saltwater mixed with sunscreen became routine and lost its romantic aura.

We used to sit at individual desks at school in Mexico. In Israel, it was two-seater desks and students seated in pairs. Territoriality was more evident, and kids drew a line in the middle so that one's neighbor's pencil did not find itself on the wrong side of the desk.

Perhaps one of the more defining elements of the context of school was, of course, the school uniform. In Mexico, we wore old-fashioned uniforms with white shirts or blouses, ties, a blazer or sweater vest with the school crest, and tailored trousers for boys and tartan skirts for girls. It was liberating to wear jeans and a blue shirt with the school symbol for school in Israel. The situation was generally more liberated, and the informal uniform reflected other elements, laid-back rules, and permitted behaviors. We didn't have to stand up when the teachers walked in and remain standing until allowed to sit down.

My first Yom Kippur in Israel was perhaps the biggest eye-opener regarding context, situations, and the elements that make them up: space and its boundaries and access to it, time and people's relationship with it, objects or props, language and co-presence, roles and rules.

The country grinds to a halt on the "Day of Atonement." It is a public holiday during which most Israeli Jews refrain from driving. The driving ban is not dictated by law but is observed out of deference for the holy day, and children and secular adults take over the deserted highways on their bicycles and skateboards.

It gets oddly quiet. The buzz of traffic and honking are replaced by the voices of children calling out to each other with palpable excitement as they plan their routes that include major highways, which are theirs for 24 hours.

A surprising stillness characterizes the day. Israeli television channels stop broadcasting; there is no public transportation; stores, restaurants, and offices are closed, and most people wear white as they walk around the streets, meeting neighbors and not rushing anywhere.

All of these taken together create a situation that feels elevated from people's everyday, profane routine. Even though bike-riding is not part of a religious ritual, the religious holiday is felt by all, not just in synagogues, because the absence of cars, the white garb, and all the other conditions invest the public sphere with a measure of sanctity. The absence of this measure of sanctity is what, according to Postman (1986), makes authentic religious experience impossible on television.

> ...on television, religion, like everything else, is presented as entertainment, quite simply and without apology. Everything that makes religion a historic, profound, and sacred human activity is stripped away; there is no ritual, no dogma, no tradition, no theology, and above all, no sense of spiritual transcendence. (pp. 116–117)

One no longer has to relocate for work or immigrate to a different country to experience foreign cultures or languages. I can accompany my friends on a walk on an exotic beach in Thailand through Facetime from my living room at home. I can join a work discussion in a meeting room physically located in Tokyo and conducted in Japanese, automatically translated into Hebrew. I can live-stream my bike ride on the empty streets of Tel Aviv on Yom Kippur for my Facebook friends. However, none of these will be the same because, as Postman explains further,

> Not all forms of discourse can be converted from one medium to another. It is naive to suppose that something that has been expressed in one form can be expressed in another without significantly changing its meaning, texture, or value...We may find it convenient to send a condolence card to a bereaved friend, but we delude ourselves if we believe that our card conveys the same meaning as our broken and whispered words when we are present. The card not only changes the words but eliminates the context from which the words take their meaning. (p. 117)

We now express our condolences on people's Facebook pages for all their friends to see, in what seems like the farthest from whispered words possible. The rules of conduct that once had to be observed in that kind of situation changed along with the words' meanings, and we became definitively and absolutely blind to the original context. It is now our media of communication that create diverse cultural environments (Meyrowitz, 1986).

Postman claimed that television created a context of entertainment, and it was hard to recreate or recontextualize a screen saturated with memories of profane events as a frame for sacred events. Before and after the television evangelists' sermons came commercials and cartoons, violence, and sex. On social media, as explained before, context collapses altogether, and on our Facebook feeds, we find news item after news item about someone's demise, an ad for shoes, a dog that adopted a cat, or a man's reaction to his wife's pregnancy announcement. All of this without even the commercials between television shows or the words "now…this" (problematic themselves, as previously explained) as a transition between emotionally disparate stories on the news. All of it, of course, is based on what the algorithm has learned about us and our preferences.

These algorithms have made situations confusing, our environments toxic, and context invisible. As individuals, we can benefit from therapies such as those discussed in Chapter Ten (CBT or ACT) with their focus on the self-as-context, but to alleviate the context blindness of humanity as a whole, different tools are required. The field of inquiry called media ecology provides such tools. In his authoritative book about media ecology, Lance Strate (2017) explains that media mediate. They stand between our original conditions and ourselves, and the new conditions become our new environment. As we become conditioned to our new conditions, they become routine and taken for granted. "They recede into the background, fade from our awareness, move out of our field of selective attention and perception and become effectively invisible, essentially imperceptible, and therefore environmental" (pp. 112–113).

According to media ecology, the terms "medium" and "environment" are synonyms, and, as I believe I have made clear, so are "situation" and "context." Media ecology, then, is the study of media as environments, of environments as media—of contexts. It is the study of the structure of situations. Media ecology is context analysis.

> [It] implies looking at communication environments as systems within systems within systems. It means trying to identify the significant characteristics of each system as a whole, the subsystems of which it is composed, the larger system within which it functions, and all the significant relationships among them. To make things even more confusing, context analysis takes as its subject matter the transactions between individual and reality, individual and individual, individual and group, group and culture, culture and culture, and tries to see them all as functions of one another. Moreover, context analysis or media ecology gives special attention to the roles played in each of these transactions by the media through which they are conducted. By "medium," we

> mean any agent or agency through which two or more discrete elements are linked in a transacting system. (Postman, 2006, p. 8)

This may sound complicated, but as context analysis is a method not in the scientific sense but rather a way of studying and trying to understand the human condition, it can become an approach for all of us, laypersons and not just scholars, to understand the mediated environments we inhabit and raise awareness of what they are turning us into. The tools for analysis are mostly questions we should ask to bring media, technology, and their effects out of their transparency, or in Postman's (1986) terms, based on Roland Barthes', to uncover that they have become mythic—the common and dangerous tendency to think of our technological creations as if they were God-given, as if they were a part of the natural order of things rather than artifacts produced in a specific political and historical context.

A more complete description and discussion of these questions can be found in Strate's book (2017), but the following provides a basis or a general idea of what we look for when analyzing context. Some of Postman's (1999, pp. 42-53) questions are:

1. What is the problem to which this technology is a solution?
2. Whose problem is it?
3. Which people and what institutions might be most seriously harmed by a technological solution?
4. What new problems might be created because we have solved this problem?
5. What sort of people and institutions might acquire special economic and political power because of technological change?
6. What changes are being enforced by new technologies, and what is being gained and lost by such changes?

Elsewhere, Postman (2000) asks:

1. To what extent does a medium contribute to the uses and development of rational thought?
2. To what extent does a medium contribute to the development of democratic processes?
3. To what extent do new media give greater access to meaningful information?
4. To what extent do new media enhance or diminish our moral sense, our capacity for goodness?
5. What is the relationship between innovation and communication, technology, and moral progress?

Based on Erving Goffman's concept of situations, Nystrom's questions (in Strate, 2017, p. 232) about communication environments are:

1. What systems does the situation function within?
2. What are the temporal boundaries of the situation?
3. What are the spatial boundaries of the situation?
4. How are the boundaries of the situation marked?
5. Are the boundaries of the situation relatively fixed or relatively flexible?
6. Are the boundaries of the situation relatively permeable or impermeable?
7. What are the front and back regions of the performance?
8. How does behavior differ in front and back regions?

Finally, in his talk about media ecology as part of a series about schools of thought in communication hosted by Universidad Carlos III in Madrid, Strate ends with a few other questions that media ecology encourages us to ask. Some of them are:

1. How do media of communication affect our ability for rational thought and our emotional lives?
2. How does it affect the use of our senses? And our ability to focus?
3. How is our sense of time and space influenced by media?
4. What happens to our consciousness and our roles and relationships?
5. Do dialogue and conversation change? And how?
6. And what happens to our sense of identity?

Strate ends this series of questions with a call to wake up and pay attention to the present. Mindfulness, if you will. CBT or ACT, but for culture or even humanity. What is this, if not a call to maintain our ability to see and understand context?

These questions revolve around media characteristics such as durability, portability, speed of transmission, temporal and spatial biases, volume, and symbolic form, all of which contribute to social biases and epistemological biases, and when it comes to our most recent technologies—those at the heart of this book—interactivity and automation.

I hope it is clear by now that what I have attempted in this book is to answer some of these questions, to engage in context analysis of the contextual technologies that are making us context-blind. The analysis began with the human capabilities that these technologies have extended and those they have amputated. It then continued with a discussion of the environment of social media, location, and sensors, and how they have shaped our behavior.

I disagree with Strate (2017, p. 203), who believes that new media are part of the evolution of the electronic media environment and that their key characteristics have been at least potentially present in the earliest forms of electric technology. I am one of the media ecologists he mentions who consider digital technologies to represent an entirely new kind of media environment, one that has made us blind to context. It is a sea change.

Caetextia, or the context blindness of people with autism as a glimpse into our human future, is at the center of the following concluding chapter.

References

Malinowski, B. (1923). *The problem of meaning in primitive languages. The meaning of meaning.* New York: Harcourt, Brace.

Meyrowitz, J. (1986). *No sense of place: The impact of electronic media on social behavior.* New York: Oxford University Press.

Postman, N. (1986). *Amusing ourselves to death: Public discourse in the age of show business.* New York: Penguin.

Postman, N. (1999). *Building a bridge to the eighteenth century: How the past can improve our future.* New York: Alfred Knopf.

Postman, N. (2000, June). The humanism of media ecology. In *Proceedings of the Media Ecology Association* (Vol. 1, No. 1, pp. 10–16).

Postman, N. (2006). Media ecology education. *Explorations in Media Ecology*, *5*(1), 5–14.

Strate, L. (2017). *Media ecology: An approach to understanding the human condition.* New York: Peter Lang.

Wittgenstein, L. (1958). *Philosophical investigations* (2nd ed.). Oxford: Blackwell.

Conclusion

Prognosis: *Homo Caetextus*—The Next Stage of Human Evolution

A few noteworthy and seemingly unconnected events happened over the last few weeks of my writing of this book. Naomi Osaka shocked the sports world when she withdrew from the French Open after avoiding requisite press appearances to concentrate on her mental health, Simone Biles withdrew from the Tokyo Olympics due to mental health concerns, and Bo Burnham's special *Inside* was released on Netflix.

Bo Burnham's career began when he was 16 years old, and he uploaded to YouTube a song he performed from his bedroom. The song got over 10 million views. At the age of almost 30, he made *Inside* from the confines of his guesthouse during the COVID-19 pandemic. *Inside* is an encapsulation of all of the symptoms of context-blind humans. It is about Internet culture, "that digital space that gave him a career and fostered a damaging anxiety disorder that led him to quit performing live comedy after 2015" (Renfro, 2021).

During the last 15 minutes of his previous show, *Make Happy*, Burnham talks to the audience about how his comedy performances are almost always about performing because he thinks people are always performing for one another.

> They say it's like the 'me' generation. It's not. The arrogance is taught, or it was cultivated. It's self-conscious. That's what it is. It's conscious of self. Social media—it's just the market's answer to a generation that demanded to perform, so the market said,

> here, perform. Perform everything to each other, all the time for no reason. It's prison. It's horrific. (Schulman, 2018)

It is indeed horrific, and the results are manifesting themselves everywhere: from Gen Zers' reluctance to answer the phone to artists not performing and athletes withdrawing from international competitions and events for which they spent years preparing. In the real world, they are withdrawing from the limelight—the intense white light focused on them. They are quite comfortable with the eye-straining, short-wavelength, high-energy blue light of their computer screens and digital devices in the mediated world.

From the cracked-open door towards the end of *Inside*, it seems like sunlight is coming in from outside, warm, and soft, and inviting. But after a year inside, Burnham goes out to a fluorescent circle, following him around to the loud laughter of an audience. What should be music to a comedian's ears is now a terrifying sound, and he can't get back inside.

Context collapses. There is no inside or outside anymore. When one performs all the time, context is lost, as there is no distinction between the stage and behind-the-scenes, and this is profoundly exhausting.

At the beginning of the film, Burnham says he's been a little depressed, but "look," he adds, "I made you some content." Indeed, he makes clear what he thinks of the buzzword by providing plenty of content himself: Content about a white woman's Instagram that is a sequence of silly photos of "latte foam art, tiny pumpkins, and fuzzy, comfy socks," and posts about trauma and loss. Content that shows him reacting to his reaction of his reaction of a piece of video. Much content is in the form of songs. One is called "That Funny Feeling," and in it is a line about Googling "derealization" and hating what you find. Derealization is the feeling that one is looking at oneself from outside one's body and feeling that things around us aren't real. Another song is called "Welcome to the Internet," where everyone shares opinions about everything, and Bo wants them all to shut up. Yet another song is called "All Eyes on Me."

The words COVID-19 or coronavirus are never mentioned. Burnham only tells the audience that just as he was getting ready to go back to performing live after years of anxiety, "something funny happened." It is not coincidental that the pandemic never comes up because it is not COVID-19 that has closed people in. It is fear of the world outside of our screens.

It is rare for a boomer to experience life online the way millennials and Gen Zers do. For a few days, though, I got a glimpse of what it feels like. A young colleague created a TikTok channel for our school and asked faculty members to think of ideas for short videos about critical thinking. Really. I'm not kidding. My thoughts passed the test of TikTok-ability, and the students in charge of production, notably versed in the medium, arranged for about two hours of shooting at various places on campus. They also asked me to bring four different outfits. The purpose of all this variety of locations and looks was to have enough material to work with when editing and end up with a dynamic, jumpy, non-monotonic 60-second video.

They liked the result. I was embarrassed and hoped nobody would see it, ever, but I came away from the experience with yet another insight into life in a decontextualized world. TikTok is all about discontinuity. Long gone are the days of the 180-degree rule in film to achieve continuity. When the point is to show changing wardrobes, props, hair, and makeup and the jump cut is the editing technique of choice, script supervisors may be out of a job soon too. Continuity is context, and we are context-blind.

Even though my colleague's intentions were excellent, and she understands what marketing to prospective students requires these days much better than I do, TikTok is probably the last medium suitable for teaching or even exposing audiences to critical thinking. TikTok is where the dumb feuds take place between Gen Z and millennials. A few months ago, Gen Zers were "canceling" millennials on TikTok, obviously not for anything profound or significant, but the older generation's fashion choices and tastes and their use of emoji. TikTok videos featured Zers burning skinny jeans, and laughing emoji were banned from their feeds, as they found them a little creepy. It turns out butterfly tops and straight-leg jeans are in now. Millennials responded with insults of their own: "The same people that are telling us we can't wear skinny jeans, or a side part, are the same people who were eating Tide pods and can't write in cursive" (Tempesta, 2021). In turn, some Gen Zers wondered if millennials were starting "their slow descent into boomerhood" (Mahan, 2021). Not much critical thinking there because there cannot be critical thinking without context, and TikTok is its own context.

In an article about why schools should not teach general critical thinking skills, the author (Hendrick, 2016) explains that at the heart of the job of an air-traffic controller,

> is a cognitive ability called "situational awareness" that involves the continuous extraction of environmental information and integrating this information with prior knowledge to form a coherent mental picture. Vast amounts of fluid information must be held in mind, and, under extreme pressure, life-or-death decisions are made across rotating 24-hour work schedules. So stressful and mentally demanding is the job that, in most countries, air traffic controllers are eligible for early retirement. In the United States, they must retire at 56 without exception.

In a series of experiments on their mental capacities conducted in the 1960s, researchers wanted to determine if the controllers had a general enhanced ability to keep track of several things at once and whether that skill could be applied to other situations. The experiments found that the air-traffic controllers did no better than anyone else when tested on various skills outside their own area of expertise. Their remarkably sophisticated cognitive abilities did not translate beyond their professional area.

Based on the findings of these experiments, the author claims that schools are trying, in vain in his view, to teach students a set of generalized critical thinking skills and problem-solving approaches that can be applied to every area. Schools are doing this because they believe that students will require these skills and approaches to flourish in the job market.

Critical thinking is a crucial component in students' future success, but it cannot be detached from context. Suppose they don't know anything about Don Quixote de la Mancha. In that case, it is an exercise in futility, like tilting at windmills, to try to teach them to analyze situations and gain perspective about themselves by using the idea of tilting at windmills.

My school's TikToks on critical thinking are fun examples of lies debunked, commonplaces questioned, and clichés exposed. They do not and cannot teach how to spot fake news generally or refute stereotypes. By the time one is done saying "critical thinking," the next suggested video has appeared to the tune of "Peaches" by Justin Bieber.

For example, to teach critical thinking about nudity and the difference between erotic art, pornography, and documentary or photojournalistic nudity, context is essential, and context is scarce. Facebook—the millennial cousin of Gen Z's TikTok—took down a post by the Anne Frank Center for showing nude Holocaust victims. The photograph in question depicts a group of naked, emaciated children, triggering Facebook's nudity policy. This was not the first such incident. Without context, another image involving nudity—the iconic news photograph from the Vietnam War of a naked nine-year-old girl fleeing a napalm strike—was blocked in 2016. They were both later restored by Facebook, citing their historical importance.

After years of living on social media, we have lost sight of context in the real world. More and more, it appears that we can all benefit from the Social Stories used to help people with autism navigate the social world (Vermeulen, 2011). As previously described, Social Stories are not about social skills in general, but rather are built around specific contexts. For example, when the person who arrives is a close family member, you kiss them and say "hi." When the person who arrives is not an immediate family member, you shake hands and say "hi." Social competence requires more than social skills; it demands contextual sensitivity—something difficult for people with autism—and, progressively, all people.

The term "socially appropriate behavior" is misleading unless the context is specified; socially appropriate behavior in one situation might be inappropriate in another. Social competence is not about knowing whether a particular behavior is socially proper; it is the knowledge of when that behavior is suitable and when it is not.

High-functioning people with autism know many social rules, but they have difficulty adapting these rules to changing contexts or making exceptions to them. A generic social skill such as how to start a conversation is not helpful if the difference in context between a doctor's waiting room and a bar with friends is not attached to that skill. Social contexts or situations need to be understood first, and only then can rules and behavior be attached to each context.

A classroom, for example, is a particular space with specific props, including chairs, desks, and a whiteboard. The professor and the students are co-present in it. Classes in classrooms start and end at specific times. If students understood the social context of a classroom, they would then understand that the rules of behavior don't include walking in late holding balloons and singing "Happy Birthday" to a friend.

In the introduction to this book, I explained that some characteristics of context blindness, as described by autism experts, resemble those of the average technology-using human. I then asked whether people with autism could be giving us a glimpse into the broader human condition—whether it is possible that technology-driven context blindness is itself partially responsible for the explosion in autism spectrum disorder diagnoses. Could this be a case of humans driving our own evolution with our technology?

It seems like the answer to all these questions is "yes." The difference between people with autism and the rest of us is a matter of degree. Most of us may still be regarded as neurotypical, but the number of people diagnosed with autism has been growing. That is why it is a spectrum and why we talk about neurodiversity of neurotypical and neurodivergent people. As Enriquez and Gullans (2015) suggest, we may be evolving ourselves or driving our own evolution with our inventions, our media, our technologies, etc. As they explain, we have redesigned our world and our bodies while at the same time becoming an ever more domesticated and smarter species. However, taking control of our evolution can also generate surprises. The symptoms of this rapid evolution include, among other things, explosions in allergies, obesity, and autism.

The authors use a clever acronym, DESTINY, to describe the six environmental stimuli propelling evolution and that we adapt to every day, with short-term and long-term consequences. The "d" stands for diet, and it includes calories, protein, fats, micronutrients, and vitamins, and alters our bodies and what lives within us. The "e" is the most relevant of the stimuli to the thesis of this book. It stands for an enriched environment full of music, toys, puzzles, schooling, information, and media, all of which rearrange children's developing brains.

The "s" stands for the types of stress we live with today that are very different from those of our ancestors. They were less healthy than we are, and we eat better than they did, but they didn't multitask and didn't have to do so much and so fast.

The "t" is for toxins, which are far more widespread today than they ever were. "I" is for infections that alter and recode our genes. "N" stands for nurture—how we care for and raise our young, which is very different from what it was like in traditional tribal settings.

The "y" stands for "you" and your offspring—all of us—not only the recipients of these stimuli but also their drivers. Evolution doesn't simply "happen" to us anymore. We are driving our fast evolution in unnatural ways. Enriquez and Gullans (2015) explain:

> As we alter our outside world, the outside world, in turn, can alter our bodies, our four genomes, and that of future generations through at least three core evolutionarily conserved biological systems: The hormones and growth factors released by our endocrine system alter the functions and genomes throughout our bodies during our lives. The nervous system wires and directs neurotransmitters. And our immune system deploys its various weapons…The seven DESTINY stimuli, acting via or in response to these three systems, transmit events and conditions around us to our genomes, leaving memories that can linger across generations. (n.p.)

The world we live in with its abundance of calories, pesticides, lead paint, urban life, and sixteen hours of light (but little of it sunlight), stimulates and challenges our bodies in ways that earlier humans never experienced. These challenges lead to phenomena such as allergies that are one of the indications of our evolving bodies. Never before in history have we had so many allergies and so many allergic people, and this is not due to society becoming more aware of them and better at diagnosing them.

There are various hypotheses to explain the rise in allergies, including that we may have tipped the balance a bit too far, and that some of what has made our lives cleaner and safer has had unintended consequences.

Like Enriquez and Gullans, I cannot remember anyone asking dinner guests in the past, before sitting down at the table, if they had any allergies. Today, the overwhelming prevalence of allergies, combined with the fear of lawsuits, led Dunkin' Donuts to post a (literal) trigger warning: "Dear Valued Customers: Please be advised that any of our products may contain allergens."

Clear signs and traces of the species we are becoming can be found in what is popular or trending on social media. Social media have not made the allergies themselves worse, but they have certainly played a role in how we handle the social aspects of food allergies: preschools that ban birthday cakes over fears of allergies, food allergy bullying, food allergy triggers at schools, and tips for nailing an awesome allergy-friendly kids' party.

As with every other harbinger of our rapid, human-driven evolution, obesity is always a trending topic on social media, and #bodyshaming and #bodypositive are popular hashtags. The obesity epidemic is another sign of our changing species. According to the World Health Organization (WHO, 2021), worldwide obesity has nearly tripled since 1975. In 2016, more than 1.9 billion adults 18 years and older were overweight. Of these, over 650 million were obese. In other words, 39 % of adults aged 18 years and over were overweight, and 13 % were obese. Thirty-nine million children under the age of five were overweight or obese in 2020. Over 340 million children and adolescents aged 5–19 were overweight or obese in 2016. Most of the world's population lives in countries where being overweight or obese kills more people than being underweight.

One popular explanation has been super-sized soft drinks and fast food, but too much food has combined with lack of physical activity. Machines have replaced muscles, jobs have stopped requiring physical activity, and in rural areas, hard manual labor has been reduced by the adoption of tractors, combines, mowers, and pickup trucks. Stress and sleeplessness have contributed as well, and it seems that the only thing the creators of *Wall-E* got wrong was the timeline.

The "e" in DESTINY—the environmental stimuli that are propelling evolution—stands for our enriched environment, by which Enriquez and Gullans mean media and technology. In their discussion of what they call robots, and I call contextual technologies throughout this book, the authors begin with the idea that robots perform any given task at least an order of magnitude better than average humans.

> Twice as many aircraft accidents are now due to pilot error as opposed to mechanical or autopilot failure. Automation and human-robot coexistence have driven the chances of dying on a commercial flight down to 1 in 45 million. Pilots will touch the controls less and less, until eventually, a flight becomes like the trains one takes from terminal to terminal in an airport. (n.p.)

They also discuss the automated (or contextually aware) features that car designers and companies are incorporating into new models, such as collision avoidance, self-parking, lane maintenance, and adaptive cruise control. All these are making human drivers anachronistic.

Resonating with one of the media ecological concepts that opened this book (that abilities delegated to media tend to atrophy), Enriquez and Gullans add:

> Why is this relevant to overall human evolution? Because we are gradually getting very, very used to living side by side with robots, needing them, improving them, holding them in our hands, and even implanting them. There is increasing need and pressure to interface with, use, and integrate robots into our daily lives, internally and externally. Short-term, what we do daily, for how long, and with whom, is likely to change in a similar way to how mechanized agriculture changed the habits, landscape, and bodyscape of millions. Abrupt changes in physical labor patterns, physical abilities that evolved over hundreds of thousands of years that are suddenly useless, can have real consequences. (n.p.)

My thesis here is that the most fateful consequences of these technologies are cognitive as well as physical. Among them, most significantly, is context blindness or *caetextia*—"the most dominant manifestation of autistic behavior at the highest levels of the autistic spectrum" (Caetextia, 2009a).

According to Enriquez and Gullans (2015),

> Conditions and diseases develop and spread at different rates. A rapid spike in air-borne or waterborne infectious diseases like the flu or cholera is tragic but normal. A rapid spike in what was thought to be a genetic condition, like autism, is abnormal; when you see the latter, it is reasonable to think something has really changed, and not for the better. Autism is diagnosed in 1 percent of individuals in Asia, Europe, and North America, and 2.6 percent of South Koreans. (n.p.)

We know there is a strong genetic component to autism, but the complete picture is still unclear. The hundreds of gene mutations identified so far do not explain most of today's cases and based on studies with large numbers of children and adults (Sandin et al., 2014), we also know that along with genetics, environmental factors are driving more and more autism cases.

> We have taken a disease we mostly inherited and rapidly turned it into a condition we can trigger...The rapid pace of today's human-driven evolution may not be giving humanity time to adapt and to reach a steady-state within a new environment. Autism may be just one harbinger, one symptom of our radically changing world. Almost every aspect of human life has changed—moving from rural to urban; living in an antiseptic environment; eating very different sugars, fats, and preservatives; experiencing novel man-made stimuli; ingesting large quantities of medicines and chemicals; being sedentary and living indoors. Given so many transformations, it would be surprising if our bodies and brains did not change as a result. (Enriquez and Gullans, 2015, n.p.)

With our technologies, we have become an ever more dominant species, but our ability to shape today's planet does not guarantee our long-term survival.

Often there are unintended, ignored, and unknown consequences to what we do and choose.

One of the major ignored consequences is global warming, and as I write the last few pages of this book in the summer of 2021, it seems we have pushed the planet past its final tipping point (Haque, 2021). It is now hotter in the eastern United States than it is in Pakistan. London recently got more than a month's worth of rain in a few minutes. There have been unprecedented rains followed by deadly flooding in central China and whole areas of Germany, drought in North America, and wildfires in the sub-Arctic. California is burning again. Temperatures in Canada have reached 120 Fahrenheit (49 Celsius), Finland and Ireland have experienced tropical heat, and the Siberian tundra is ablaze. It all feels off the charts this summer, and these extreme events have surprised scientists in how suddenly frequent they are. They have been predicting weather disruption from climate change for decades, but the speed with which these extremes have been hitting has taken them by surprise.

This is global warming we can feel. We can see what is meant by the Anthropocene with our own eyes. I am bewildered by the question of why we have not tried to slash carbon emissions, find ways to restore the ice sheets, and revive the great forests instead of dreaming of life on Mars or the Metaverse.

While it is not an official geological era, the Anthropocene is defined by human activity, leading to the destruction of natural ecosystems, loss of biodiversity, and climate change. Plants and animals are responding to human pressure. Some bird species are forgetting to migrate, and there are mosquito breeds that have adapted specifically to subway tunnels. Backyard bird feeders are behind alterations in the shape and strength of the beak of house finches. Some mammals are becoming nocturnal to prevent encounters with humans. Swallows are developing smaller wings to help them evade buildings and cars. Fish are growing mouths that are smaller and harder to hook. "It's a mistake to think evolution requires millennia" (Weber, 2018).

We are one of the primary drivers of environmental change, and we might be "the world's greatest evolutionary force, frequently driving what is now called 'rapid evolution', 'contemporary evolution' or 'evolution on ecological time scales'" (Hendry et al., 2017).

The human footprint on our planet should be evident to all, but it is not because we are context-blind. With our instruments, our media, our technology, we have mastered more and more of our environment and guided it toward our own purposes.

Enriquez and Gullans (2015) claim that we have changed our world to such an extent that we are witnessing evolution in real time and birthing our successor species. Our great-grandchildren may be a species very different from us, they say, as we are transitioning as a species into a *Homo Evolutis*.

The question, of course, is what we will do next. Will we slow down this transition? Can we regain some sight? In the last chapter of *Technopoly*, Neil Postman (1992) talks about the question that cultural critics are always asked: What is the solution to the problems you describe? He adds that critics seldom like the question because in most cases, they are entirely satisfied with themselves for having posed the problem and, in any event, are rarely skilled in formulating practical suggestions about anything.

I cannot say that I am satisfied with having posed the problem. It is a problem of such magnitude that posing it is a source of great sadness. Moreover, I have attempted to provide a solution by suggesting context analysis as the media ecological approach to our human condition, but I must be honest and admit that I doubt it is a viable solution.

Media ecologists maintain that context is the key to understanding media and defending ourselves from their detrimental effects. For example, McLuhan (in Strate, 2014) explains that our media and technology function as environments fading into the background as they become routine and therefore invisible to us. That,

> in order to bring them back into conscious awareness, we need to find anti-environments or counter-environments, whose bias runs counter to those of the prevailing environment, thereby providing us with a vantage point from which to objectively observe and assess our main environment and find the patterns that may allow us to escape the Maelstrom or Tempest. (pp. 143–144)

To have a vantage point is to have perspective. It implies the ability to see the larger picture. To observe and assess an environment means possessing the ability to understand context. I would love nothing better than to join Postman (1992) in his recommendation to become technological resistance fighters. As he defines them, resistance fighters are people who understand:

> that technology must never be accepted as part of the natural order of things, that every technology is a product of a particular economic and political context and carries with it a program, an agenda, and a philosophy that may or may not be life-enhancing and that therefore require scrutiny, criticism, and control. In short, a technological resistance fighter maintains an epistemological and psychic distance from any technology so that it always appears somewhat strange, never inevitable, never natural. (pp. 184–185)

Unfortunately, I am not sure we can be resistance fighters, as we have delegated to technology those capabilities too: to maintain distance, get perspective, and understand context. Technology is entirely natural and inevitable in our minds.

Lance Strate (2014) is right. The key to avoiding technological dystopia is context. We need to find "the appropriate contexts for the specific purposes we have in mind, the appropriate medium for the kinds of communication we wish to engage in, the appropriate environment for living a fully human life" (p. 145). But I don't know if this is possible. We are *Homo caetextus*. It may be too late.

References

Enriquez, J., & Gullans, S. (2015). *Evolving ourselves: How unnatural selection and nonrandom mutation are changing life on earth*. New York: Portfolio/Penguin.

Haque, U. (July 17, 2021). Is this the beginning of runaway global warming? *Eand*. https://eand.co/is-this-the-beginning-of-runaway-global-warming-ba472b9143c8

Hendrick, C. (December 5, 2016). Why schools should not teach general critical-thinking skills. *Aeon*. https://aeon.co/ideas/why-schools-should-not-teach-general-critical-thinking-skills

Hendry, A. P., Gotanda, K. M., & Svensson, E. I. (2017). Human influences on evolution and the ecological and societal consequences. *Philosophical Transactions of the Royal Society of London. Series B, Biological Sciences*, *372*(1712). doi:10.1098/rstb.2016.0028

Mahan, L. (February 26, 2021). The dumb Internet feud between Gen Z and Millennials, explained by a Gen-Zer. *Insidehook*. https://www.insidehook.com/article/internet/infighting-gen-z-millennials-explained

Postman, N. (1992). *Technopoly: The surrender of culture to technology*. New York: Alfred Knopf.

Renfro, K. (June 12, 2021). 31 details you might have missed in Bo Burnham's 'Inside.' *Insider*. https://www.insider.com/bo-burnham-inside-special-details-analysis-breakdown-2021-6

Sandin, S., Lichtenstein, P., Kuja-Halkola, R., Larsson, H., Hultman, C. M., & Reichenberg, A. (2014). The familial risk of autism. *Jama*, *311*(17), 1770–1777.

Schulman, M. (June 25, 2018). Bo Burnham's age of anxiety. *The New Yorker*. https://www.newyorker.com/magazine/2018/07/02/bo-burnhams-age-of-anxiety

Strate, L. (2014). *Amazing ourselves to death: Neil Postman's brave new world revisited*. New York: Peter Lang.

Tempesta, E. (February 5, 2021). The generational war continues! *The Daily Mail*. https://www.dailymail.co.uk/femail/article-9229583/Millennials-war-Gen-Z-skinny-jeans-parts.html

Vermeulen, P. (November/December, 2011). Autism: From mind blindness to context blindness. *The Neurotypical*. https://www.theneurotypical.com/context-blindness.html

Weber, B. (November 15, 2018). Humans are having huge influence on evolution of species, study says. *CBC*. https://www.cbc.ca/news/science/humans-evolution-1.4906534

WHO. (June 9, 2021). *Obesity and overweight*. World Health Organization. https://www.who.int/news-room/fact-sheets/detail/obesity-and-overweight

INDEX

A

B

C

D

H

I

S

U

V

W

Y

Z

UNDERSTANDING
MEDIA
ECOLOGY

Lance Strate
General Editor

This series is devoted to scholarship relating to media ecology, a field of inquiry defined as the study of media as environments. Within this field, the term "medium" can be defined broadly to refer to any human technology or technique, code or symbol system, invention or innovation, system or environment. Media ecology scholarship typically focuses on how technology, media, and symbolic form relate to communication, consciousness, and culture, past, present and future. This series is looking to publish research that furthers the formal development of media ecology as a field; that brings a media ecology approach to bear on specific topics of interest, including research and theoretical or philosophical investigations concerning the nature and effects of media or a specific medium; that includes studies of new and emerging technologies and the contemporary media environment as well as historical studies of media, technology, and modes and codes of communication; scholarship regarding technique and the technological society; scholarship on specific types of media and culture (e.g., oral and literate cultures, image, etc.), or of specific aspects of culture such as religion, politics, education, journalism, etc.; critical analyses of art and popular culture; and studies of how physical and symbolic environments function as media.

For additional information about this series or for the submission of manuscripts, please contact:

Lance Strate, Series Editor | *strate@fordham.edu*

To order other books in this series, please contact our Customer Service Department:

peterlang@presswarehouse.com (within the U.S.)
orders@peterlang.com (outside the U.S.)

Or browse online by series:

www.peterlang.com

www.ingramcontent.com/pod-product-compliance
Ingram Content Group UK Ltd.
Pitfield, Milton Keynes, MK11 3LW, UK
UKHW020842290926
15470UKWH00004B/1496

9 781433 186134